the collected home

the collected home

ROOMS WITH STYLE, GRACE, AND HISTORY

darryl carter

WITH TRISH DONNALLY
PHOTOGRAPHS BY GORDON BEALL

CLARKSON POTTER/PUBLISHERS
NEW YORK

Published in the United States by Clarkson Potter/Publishers, an
imprint of the Crown Publishing Group, a division of Random
House, Inc., New York.
www.crownpublishing.com
www.clarksonpotter.com

CLARKSON POTTER is a trademark and POTTER with colophon
is a registered trademark of Random House, Inc.

Library of Congress Cataloging-in-Publication Data
Carter, Darryl
    The collected home/Darryl Carter with Trish Donnally.—1st ed.
       p.   cm.
    Includes index.
1. Interior decoration—Psychological aspects.   I. Donnally, Trish.
II. Title.
    NK2113.C365   2012
    747—dc23   2011043291

ISBN 978-0-307-95394-0

Printed in China

Book and jacket design by Rae Ann Spitzenberger
Jacket photographs by Gordon Beall

JACKET IMAGE: Artwork by Edward Finnegan hangs above my
client's coffee table that was enlarged to better suit the space through
an engineering marvel performed by Joe Wills. His work included
matching the cleft edge of the existing table—it is as if it was always
at its current size. The chair was found during one of my many travels.

10 9 8 7 6 5 4 3 2 1

First Edition

To my parents—and all parents—who
have found themselves with children prone
to unusual paths. Thank you for so much
belief and continued support.

JACKSON, FOUR, WAS HANDED A CHILDREN'S MENU TO COLOR
DURING DINNER. HE PROMPTLY FLIPPED IT OVER TO THE BLANK
SIDE DECLARING, "I WOULD RATHER DRAW THAN COLOR."

ROMAN, THREE, TAPPED HIS HAND AGAINST A NINETEENTH-CENTURY
CORINTHIAN COLUMN IN WASHINGTON, DC, AND PROCLAIMED, "NOT REAL."
HIS FIRST EXPERIENCE WITH CLASSICAL ARCHITECTURE HAD BEEN, OF COURSE,
THE TROPHÉE DES ALPES, BUILT IN 6 BC FOR EMPEROR AUGUSTUS.

CONTENTS

PROLOGUE

The horse sculpture in the foyer of my Washington home is my most prized possession. It profoundly speaks to the essence of my work and the concept of this book. The horse greets you upon entering, and so begins the story of my collected home.

In collecting your own home, you are sharing the story of your life. The furniture, art, colors, textures, sounds, and scents all convey details about your character, sense of humor, and experiences. Ironically, while our homes hold so much promise to be our sanctuaries, they have somehow progressively become an aside in our daily lives. The making of a home seems to be increasingly thought of as a chore that is managed through common catalog offerings and compulsive purchases informed by immediate need.

COLLECTIONS
SHOULD SPEAK TO
YOU OR OF YOU.

As I see it, the home should be a collected assemblage of treasures meaningful to the homeowner. I believe it is better to have an empty room than an instant room. Forgo the immediate, and embrace the lasting. This is the guiding principle for collecting a home.

My home speaks to me. It is a gathering of all things personal—each with its own story, not because of its worth, but because of its interest. I enjoy playing docent, walking guests through this view into my life. It is a veritable unfolding tale of journeys, passions, and cherished gifts. Each object captured my attention because of its humor, complexity, utility, innovation, or sentimentality. Some rare, some common—ready for reinvention through a coat of paint or reupholstery, each acquired from antiques dealers, architectural reclamation, flea markets, or artisans' studios. These overall collections have become quite a gathering, evoking fond memories and providing a view into just how my mind works. So many stories, so much reinvention. I love sharing these anecdotes with my guests, hearing their laughter and seeing their surprise.

The horse sculpture exemplifies this philosophy and represents a culmination of an odyssey of events that somehow landed it in my foyer. I was in Venice for a design summit, where I met a host of brilliant people, including Steve and Brooke Giannetti. We were on a boat bound for the Palazzo Venier dei Leoni, now home to the Peggy Guggenheim Collection.

Through the course of our conversation, Steve mentioned that I might appreciate a visit to Giannetti's Studio, which is just outside of Washington, near where my firm is based. As it turns out, his family owns a highly regarded ornamental plaster works studio spanning three generations.

On my return, a visit ensued, and thus began the pilgrimage to the horse. The studio was a warren of beautiful objects. It is one of the few remaining studios that practices bygone plaster methods, having restored many of the most important buildings in Washington. There I was overcome with architectural models and prototypical miniatures of familiar monuments, fragments of buildings, columns, cornices, and the horse. This sculpture is said to be the infrastructure reference for a bronze by Paul Wayland Bartlett, an American sculptor who worked on several of the equestrian statues that grace the traffic circles of Washington, as well as many public spaces worldwide.

The tale of the craft involved in the making of a bronze so struck me that this noble creature eventually found a home in my foyer. The Giannettis' final parting with the horse was more inspired by their want for it to fall into kindred stewardship than by a desire for monetary return. This magnificent object, which I am so fortunate to have in my home, speaks to me in every possible way. It defines the making of an object with exacting care, which should be the foundation when collecting your home and one we will explore throughout this book.

As for the horse, yes, it does have an equally extraordinary head, which I keep safely sequestered. Displaying the horse in its full context would be far too obvious.

RECLAIMED FOUNTAIN IN MY
WASHINGTON, DC, FOYER.

INTRODUCTION

Collecting all of the furnishings, finishings, and art to decorate your home should be fun, and this book is written in that spirit. Embrace and enjoy the process. The objects you collect, both expected and otherwise, are what will distinguish and define your home as an expression of you. After so much positive response to my book *The New Traditional*, I wanted to explore in more depth the essence of what brings a home to life.

For me, the key to this process is in how all of the design elements are brought together to create a harmonious whole. The home should be your refuge, a place of tranquillity. Just as you may curate a small group of prized belongings, look at your whole home and its design as a collection of objects and stories. When making design decisions, select things that are dear and personally impactful. This should be the guiding principle for all aspects of the home, from an antique door knocker to a distinctive armoire that may hide the high-tech equipment of modern life.

It can feel intimidating to decorate a home, whether it's a small apartment, a multistory townhouse, or a grand property. The secret? Trust your instincts, and approach the process thoughtfully. This book will lead you through each of the following steps, chapter by chapter. To create something enduring, think about how you want your space to feel, and recognize the potential of the existing bones. Keep an open mind as you explore possibilities, and don't hesitate to ask for guidance. Anticipate your needs and create a plan with both short- and long-term goals. Consider ways to enhance the existing architectural envelope, and use paint, textiles, and textures to create seamless connections between spaces and objects. Seek the artisanal for pieces that have stories of their own that will enhance the dialogue of the whole house. Embellish with care, and, most important, allow room for growth. Your home and collections will evolve over time. Life changes will bring new challenges, and with forethought, you can prepare your home for them.

As you embrace this evolution, you'll gain more and more confidence in what feels right for you and your home. Prepare to discover gems when you least expect them.

I'll never forget the first time I was asked to participate in a design show house. This was my first public design venue. My room was in the center of a maze of aesthetically disparate visions, intended to collectively suggest the experience of walking through a home. Young and intimidated by the veteran designers also presenting their work, I thought,

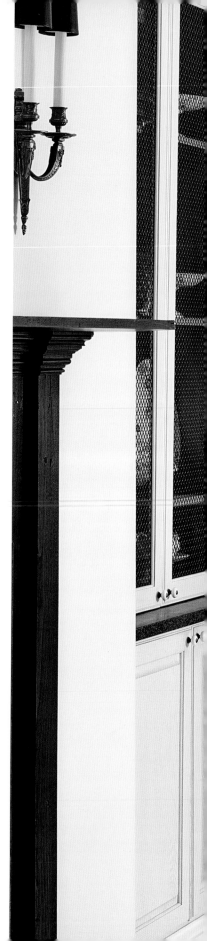

RECLAIMED
WAINSCOT
DEFINES MY
KITCHEN.

AN ANTIQUE
CANDLESNUFFER,
A RUSTIC FARM
TABLE, AND OTHER
COLLECTIBLES
HAVE MADE THIS
MY PREFERRED
CASUAL DINING
VENUE.

"This is not at all the way a home should be experienced." It felt disjointed from one space to the next; I wanted to reinvent my own room to better integrate it with the other rooms of the show house.

Just as I was completing my space the day before the opening, I suddenly felt lost. Needing some assurance, as always, I called my dear mother, who doesn't mince words at moments like these. I told her I was very concerned that my room did not feel "finished" in concert with the others. "It seems bland. I am compelled to change it. Worse yet, it is in the center of all of the adjacent rooms. It feels disappointing."

I was decorating a dining room. Having a monumental table as the centerpiece of this room has always presented a challenge, because an expansive table begs to be grounded by its endless top. I don't like oversized floral arrangements—they can block the view of others seated at the table and stifle conversation. Candles are always the go-to solution for me for adding atmosphere, but show house prohibitions would not allow candles, and certainly would not allow a fire in the fireplace. I had specified meticulous millwork for the room's walls, and then layered paint over grass cloth to make the principal wall where the fireplace was located more welcoming. Only a few pieces of unframed art hung from the walls. I commissioned a straightforward fireplace mantel with a limestone surround used on its reverse (duller) side so it would fade seamlessly into the millwork. I oxidized the andirons, fireplace poker, and tools so they would suggest use. I prefer things to have a patina rather than to look shiny and new.

AN ANTIQUE CHERRY DAYBED TOPPED WITH A RARE ADJUSTABLE BACKREST SATISFIES MY PREDILECTION FOR ARTICULATING FURNITURE. I AM INTRIGUED BY THE MECHANICS OF FURNITURE THAT MOVES.

Beneath the table, I placed an antique rug on its well-worn reverse so that its faded color would blend into the overall setting and further reinforce the approachable quality of the space. Velvet seat cushions on the chairs were muted to echo the faintest color of the rug. The space captured the intended vision, but in this moment it suddenly fell down in my mind. I convinced myself that it was too spare in relation to the other, more ornamented rooms.

"What should I do? There is no time left to change it."

My mother's words resonate to this day: "Do you feel that it's done?"

"Yes, but it looks nothing like the others," I reflected.

Once more, she asked, "Do you feel that it's done?"

"Yes, but it doesn't feel like the others."

She said with firm commitment in her tone, "You are done."

With this vote of confidence, I overcame my apprehensions and resolved to proceed as planned, although I admit, I still felt naked. The angst of the moment finally gave way to the reception, where the room was very well received. Visitors overwhelmingly congregated there for conversation. The dining room was filled with people and laughter, and the design allowed the room to be experienced as it should be.

I learned a profound lesson that has become a recurring mantra throughout my career and that I share in this book. As you begin the journey of collecting your home, don't be afraid to trust your instincts.

THE TIMEWORN QUALITY OF THESE
BELGIAN SHUTTERS APPEALS TO ME.

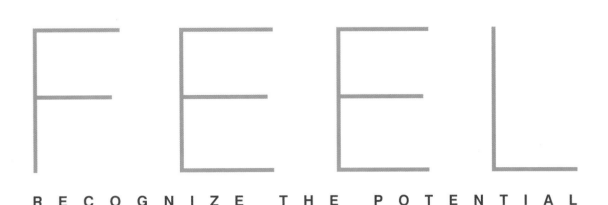

1

FEEL

RECOGNIZE THE POTENTIAL

Often, intangibles define the experience of a home. A home should be unique to the homeowner, reflective of his or her personality, lifestyle, and travels. Once you cross the threshold, something transformative should happen that distinctly makes you feel that you are at home—unlike any other environment. Your residence should welcome and embrace you, awaken your spirit, and likewise awaken the interest, curiosity, and sensory experiences of your guests. Creating this aura begins at curbside, perhaps from a cobblestone drive, and takes you into the house and out to the garden. Each of the rooms within the home should relate to the others. There must be a common sensibility.

THE PALETTE IN THIS ROOM WAS DERIVED
FROM THE COLOR AND PATINA OF THE
ORIGINAL ITALIANATE LIMESTONE MANTEL.

When I approach a design environment, my hope is that once it's done, there will be a feeling of ease and a sense of things thoughtfully collected over the passage of time. Foremost, an environment should reflect the homeowner and not the hand of a designer. Thus each object, textile, or cabinet pull is selected to suit the homeowner's lifestyle and the setting of the property. A home's decor should be highly nuance driven. Furniture pieces are critically important in a spare setting in particular, because they can't be camouflaged by too much gratuitous embellishment.

I once visited an apartment that epitomized a collected home. This occurred at an unforgettable dinner gathering in Paris that I attended as a last-minute invitee with a friend who had expatriated. I hesitated to go, because I felt I might be intruding. My friend assured me that "the more the merrier." We approached the most incredible Beaux Arts apartment building, which we entered through an antique worn limestone arch with a gate and gas lanterns. It was truly out of a storybook, so much effortless grace.

We entered the smallest gem of an apartment, where we were greeted by a gracious, welcoming host. The company turned out to be an extraordinary group of diverse guests. A royal who had come by Harley; artists dressed unabashedly as artists; politicos and professors with their students were among the mix. I have never experienced such a variety of strong personalities under one small roof. The conversation was alive with spirited opinions—yet all respectful of one another.

The environment informed the occasion. Everything was precious, yet not. Each piece of silver radiated in the glow of the red-lacquered, candlelit dining room. Layers of large, dark ancestral art gracefully defined the walls of the

THE CASUAL,
WELCOMING
SPIRIT OF THIS
LIVING ROOM
IS REINFORCED
BY THE PATINA
OF THE RUSTIC
APOTHECARY
CABINET.

space. It represented a lifetime of collecting objects, furnishings, and art, all placed as though landing where they should have over the passage of time. Nothing was too thoughtful, yet everything shared an artisanal hand. The house was alive.

This is the way a home ought to be. The experience should be welcoming and sensory, from the scent of soap in a powder room to the heft of a wooden coat hanger. Music should encourage the tilt to lively conversation. The aroma of foods should engage curiosity about a forthcoming meal. Truth be told, no matter the backdrop that I may create with a client, it is the people who finally complete the home.

There is no greater gift than the experience. Think about how your house feels, what memories it evokes, how the tactile quality of the material on a chair welcomes you to have a seat. This sense of atmosphere is not the easiest to articulate on the written page: the smell of a winter fire that lingers on into spring; the soft light cast from a candle; the scent of just-brewed coffee that wakes you in the morning or that of freshly cut grass in the afternoon. My personal penchant is the smell of cookies baking, which invariably returns me to my childhood. A home for me is least about theater or pretense. A home is brought to life by its subliminal scents and sounds, and the moments they inspire.

The highest compliment I can hope for about environments I decorate is that they are intelligent, innovative, and comfortable. When I have dinner guests, I generally place large hurricane cylinders with dense white votive candles inside them on the approach to my front door, and I dim the interior lights and light the trail of candles inside. This gesture welcomes people before the entry threshold is ever crossed.

ABOVE: A HEAVILY PATINATED NINETEENTH-CENTURY STONE TABLE RAISED ON A DOLPHIN-FORM BASE ADDS CHARACTER TO THIS GARDEN PATIO.

OPPOSITE: THE APPROPRIATENESS OF THE FRENCH LANTERNS IS INSTANTLY OBVIOUS. IN THE EVENING, THE CLOUDED HANDBLOWN GLASS CLOCHES ROMANTICALLY DIFFUSE THE DIRECT LIGHT SOURCE, GIVING THE APPEARANCE OF CANDLELIGHT.

MIX IT UP. THE CHAIRS
DO NOT NEED TO MATCH,
BUT THEY SHOULD RELATE.
ALLOW YOURSELF TO
STUMBLE UPON A PIECE
OR TWO THAT WILL SET
THE TONE FOR THE REST
OF THE FORMS.

THE CANE-BACK
SETTEE WAS
JUXTAPOSED
AGAINST A
COMMISSIONED
COMPOSITION
OF LOCAL EARTH,
PORCELAIN, AND
STONEWARE
CREATED BY
WASHINGTON
ARTIST AND MY
DEAR FRIEND
MARGARET
BOOZER.

WHITE'S CALMING EFFECT

My home is primarily white. A room that may appear at first glance to be a single shade generally consists of several shades of white that help distinguish the most subtle details of the architecture. When carefully executed, white helps create a logic and a continuity that will relate rooms seamlessly to one another. This calm palette reinforces the experience and a cohesive flow throughout the house, and against this backdrop, people and life take center stage.

Compare wool with cashmere; they may look the same at a distance, but they don't feel the same at all. Wool can feel coarse, while cashmere is supple and indulgent. I am by no means suggesting the extravagance of cashmere—rather that one textile may offer a tactile experience that another does not. One may be more suited for a bedroom and the other for a family room. An environment should feel like a warm blanket enveloping you in the winter and a cool ocean breeze washing over you in the summer. This sensuous effect is achieved through carefully selected color palettes and textiles, which we will explore in more depth later.

A cotton velvet seat cushion on a sepia-washed, cane-back settee serves as an example. This marriage of materials speaks discretely to both winter and summer. The velvet, winter—the open caning, summer; together they neutralize each other to create a perennial welcome. Placing a multimedia art piece in this setting both counterbalances and complements the demure caning. A subtle textural dialogue between the pieces emerges. Harmony results from balancing their differences.

TEXTURE PLAYS AN ESPECIALLY IMPORTANT ROLE IN A MONOCHROMATIC SETTING. IN MY BEDROOM, I CHOSE LINEN BEDDING WITH COTTON VELVET DETAILS OF A SIMILAR HUE. THIS UNEXPECTED TEXTILE PAIRING IS SUITABLE YEAR-ROUND.

It takes time, care, and effort to produce such environments. For instance, a large fallen and dried cactuslike piece of driftwood, found in the eaves of an attic on a shopping trip, profoundly inspired this oceanfront interior. The piece is responsive to both the living space and the distant ocean. For me, the abstract angle of its outstretched arms is reminiscent of the Winged Victory. Once suspended on its delicate base, it appears to float. And this otherwise overlooked castoff takes on a magnificent presence as sculpture bleached by the sun. I purposely scour some of the most unlikely venues in my constant effort to find just the right piece to bring soul to a room. This is the essence and joy of collecting your home—discovering that long-sought treasure or perhaps stumbling upon one you never even thought of that will perfectly complete the space.

TRAINING YOUR EYE: DISCOVERY

Perhaps the most obvious example of a place to find unknown treasure is in an artist's studio, replete with possibility. What inspired the commission on page 28 was a bucket of local earth, and in the distance, a vase that had been turned out of that same material. That which was a vase became three-dimensional wall art. Keep an open mind—things are never only as they first appear to be.

THIS DRIFTWOOD
ARTIFACT WAS
DISCOVERED
COVERED IN DUST
IN THE ATTIC OF AN
ANTIQUES SHOP.
I IMMEDIATELY
IMAGINED IT AS A
GRAVITY-DEFYING
CACTUSLIKE FORM.

2

COLLABORATE

UNDERSTAND SHARED GOALS

To open, in its most literal definition, means to expand, especially before the eye. This is brilliantly concise. If I had a single word to convey the spirit with which one should embrace the design of his or her home, this may be the one. If you are open to the possibilities of what your home can be, by slowly and carefully filling it with objects that are important to you, the aesthetic of your home will expand before your eyes. You may find yourself surprised at what the house tells you about itself, and more important, about yourself. Whether you are working with a professional decorator or alone, this chapter will show you how a spirit of collaboration can produce exceptional interiors.

SOMETIMES A SMALL OBJECT MAY BE
WELL PLACED ON A LARGE PEDESTAL.

Keeping an open mind when you begin a design project can be one of the biggest challenges. Prejudgment will greatly inhibit, if not defeat, the process. Through the course of my work, I have learned nothing if not to be flexible. As a beginner, I would get vexed and stay up late at night, trying to figure out how to impose my will for the good of the project, or so I thought. This thinking would have rendered me less viable as a decorator "for hire." After many collaborations, however, I've discovered that it's better to see an "obstacle" that once might have been a defeating blow as a creative challenge to be overcome. As you begin collecting your home, expanding the boundaries of the original vision can translate into an opportunity for better design.

The team at Darryl Carter and I always encourage new clients to come with as many "inspiration images" as they can manage to gather from magazines, books, and any and every other possible resource. From this we learn what speaks to them. These images guide the evolution of the design process. Most potential clients who reach out to our firm tend to be individuals who embrace the craft, time, and care necessary to make bespoke environments, where each element is thoughtfully hand selected, rather than an assemblage of stock parts that have been used in the making of so many other houses. Most clients have many great ideas in need of order and navigation. Seldom do they know with certainty what they want.

Generally we begin with a brainstorming session to determine the goals of the project. The process is one of culling ideas and refining them to determine what is most suitable, given our client's desires, space, and budget considerations. This is where I suggest you begin, too.

MY CLIENT WAS VERY
OPEN IN THE DESIGN
OF THIS PROPERTY,
AND BECAUSE OF
HIS WILLINGNESS TO
COLLABORATE, WE
ENDED UP WITH A
RARE GRANDMOTHER
CLOCK THAT
PERFECTLY SUITED
HIS WASHINGTON,
DC, APARTMENT.

AN EXTRAORDINARY "BARN DOOR" FUNCTIONS AS ART. I ALSO SUSPENDED SCULPTURE AS A LIGHT DIFFUSER—YOU MIGHT BE ABLE TO FIND UNEXPECTED LOCATIONS THROUGHOUT YOUR OWN HOME WHERE DOORS OR CEILINGS CAN PRESENT AN OPPORTUNITY FOR ART PLACEMENT.

The best projects are born of collaboration. Good relationships are open and fluid and give way to honest conversation that finally translates into these few words: "Perhaps it would be better if it were done this way." Reinventing the envelope that may have been bounded by predispositions is one of the most invigorating aspects of my work.

A FAMILY HOME

The mandate that emerged for one couple's early-twentieth-century Spanish colonial was to honor the exterior architecture. To this end, a painstaking addition was married to the original structure to appear seamless. The interior was thoughtful and artfully approached to reflect the family's lifestyle. This project became even more of a preoccupation for me when I watched this couple interact with their children. Their house clearly would be lived in by a real family. The parents told me that their children would be present in, on, and around every surface. The couple was open to unique artwork and design as long as it was child-friendly. Coffee tables might realistically be performance stages, banisters transportation; walls might be art canvases; and anything that did not defy gravity might be a projectile.

The point: Nothing could or would be too precious, and this would need to be translated into the architecture. The solutions came naturally: there would be no precious chandelier, but ceilings in the house became very dear to me, as these were opportunities to place art, out of harm's reach, in the form of laylights—glazed openings that provide natural or artificial light and that can filter light from a skylight above. I designed them as suspended light sculptures referencing origami. Doors became art, oxidized steel that would age organically over time protruded through sliding sheaths of gypsum cement. Surely these indestructible and earthen materials would be child-resistant.

A SENSE OF PLACE

I worked with my parents to help them decorate a secondary apartment in Bal Harbour, Florida. They had three must-haves: They wanted an L-shaped sofa, a flat-screen TV, and a wall of mirrors. My father also wanted dark espresso wood flooring, which incidentally is generally a favorite floor treatment of mine, but I explained to him why in this setting, which overlooks an unobstructed horizon of ocean and white beach, such a dark choice would feel foreign.

Then I dug in and got to work. I designed a lean sectional sofa suspended on intermittent dark wood L-bracket legs responsive to the architecture of the space and to what my parents wanted. Instead of camouflaging the TV, as I often do by placing it in an armoire or behind movable art, I celebrated it. Below it, I commissioned a simple ledge one foot deep by nine feet long as an architectural element to add gravity and dimension to that wall. The TV is anchored to the wall and appears to float above the ledge like a piece of art; it is also placed off center as the ledge extends much farther to the left of the TV. This makes an architectural moment out of something standard. In the dining room, I designed the mirrors as a montage of individually framed mirrors executed in a graphic rectilinear composition. A portrait installed in front of these mirrors lends a visual anchor and dimension to the space.

GEOMETRY—AND THE VIEW—WERE THE INSPIRATIONS FOR THIS DESIGN. THE LINEAR PLANES OF THE ARCHITECTURE WERE SO PURE AND THE SEASCAPE SO SIGNIFICANT THAT THE FURNITURE NEEDED TO BE INCONSPICUOUS.

THE NEED FOR A CLOSET AND THE
WANT FOR ART FIND COMPROMISE
IN THE FORM OF A NINETEENTH-
CENTURY FRENCH CELLAR DOOR.

We also collaborated on the guest bedroom regarding another goal. I always like to dedicate large expanses of walls to art. But in this room, only one wall could support a large art canvas; the opposite wall was glass, to capture the ocean views. My mother wanted another closet, for her overflow, which had to be accessed through that art wall. The closet door would have landed dead center on my would-be art moment. Of course, I had to find a solution that would give her access to the closet and still provide art for the space. In the end, I suspended a nineteenth-century French metal wine cellar door from the wall, using modern barn-door hardware. This beautiful piece both created visual interest and covered the necessary closet entry when closed.

The flooring remains one of my most memorable discussions to date. My father did not embrace what he considered the "overdesign" of the proposed flooring execution—an exaggerated diagonal chevron pattern that ran the course of the apartment. In a sparse environment, however, floors take on far greater relevance. Likewise, the floor color was very critical. The sense of place, when it is so engaged with the exterior landscape, should always be considered. Dark flooring was contrary to the logic of this environment. In this case, I must admit, I vigilantly lobbied for bleached white floors, as I didn't want to disrupt the sight line that so naturally gave way to the sandy shore of the ocean beyond.

Crafting a space with so many progressive iterations bears the sweetest fruit at the end. After pouring so much care, thought, and collaboration into the project, the single most rewarding moment is handing over the finished product. I'll never forget my father's delighted voice when he phoned me upon first arriving at the completed apartment. Entering the space is transformative. Each time I visit, I am instantly taken by the apartment's sense of calm.

THE DESIGN OF THIS BEDROOM WAS AN EXERCISE IN
RESTRAINT. WITH ITS BLEACHED WOOD FINISH, THE
BED IS INTENDED TO MELD INTO THE ARCHITECTURE.

SPEAK CANDIDLY

It never fails to surprise me that the most unlikely clients become engaged, if not fully absorbed, in the design process. These tend to be individuals who are most consumed by their professions. Yet the process, when embraced, becomes play for them. A palpable distinction exists between a micromanager and a genuinely invested client. Exploration with an open mind leads to the discovery of things none of us might have envisioned alone. The process evolves, governed only by frank discourse. I always propose what I consider the best possible solution for a space; then I collaborate with my clients to determine if my idea fits their lifestyle. If not, we talk candidly and adjust the design accordingly. It's critical that you communicate clearly and openly with your decorator, architect, or partner about the priorities of your wish list.

THE SUBTLE DETAIL OF DIAGONALLY LAID FLOORING CAN ENHANCE YOUR SPACE.

suggestions for flooring

You'll encounter a series of sidebars with hints throughout this book. Many may seem like common sense, but with the myriad details that need to be considered when collecting a home, you may find these hints helpful or at least a trigger to think about items that are easy to overlook. Though the following list may not be comprehensive, here are some details to keep in mind when updating your flooring:

- Consider installing a special padding or a cork subfloor for sound absorption. Hard surfaces on an upper level can be noisy below. Apartments often have requirements for subfloors.

- Consider installing radiant floor heating under tile floors.

- How will your flooring material be installed—will it be floating, glued down, or nailed down?

- For stone and tile, consider sealing the material to protect against dirt and grime penetrating the stone and grout.

- Specifying the direction of the flooring, if optional, can visually enhance the sense of space.

- Consider how transitions between flooring materials will occur—from hardwood to stone or tile. Think about color and finishes so that they integrate quietly.

- Consider the durability of flooring materials in high-traffic areas in the home.

NOTE: All the information offered here and in future chapters will vary in accordance with your individual scope and jurisdictional codes, so always consult the appropriate experts.

Conference Room - South

P L A N

3

When you are embarking on a design project, nothing is more important than planning. You must think forward coherently and anticipate your every need. Otherwise, you might miss irretrievable opportunities. The process may initially seem overwhelming, but the key is to plan carefully and logically, considering each and every detail while imagining yourself actually functioning in the proposed environment in your day-to-day life. How will you move about the space? How can a space be organized to work most efficiently for your needs? How, where, and with whom will you gather, both privately and in the company of guests? This foundation will influence future decoration.

CONSIDER EVERY DETAIL

As my design associates and I begin a relationship with our clients, we spend a tremendous amount of time in discovery. That means trying to understand all that is important to their daily lives. During this information-gathering process, we also assemble the team that will finally bring the project to fruition. Depending on its scope, the players may include an architect, a general contractor, and a host of tradespeople, landscape architects, and other experts. Given the possible number of players, information management is key. Mistakes may happen, but they can be significantly minimized by a disciplined process.

With this chapter, I'd like to give you an insider's tour of how this planning process really unfolds in professional hands, so you can apply it to collecting your home. It begins with a realistic self-assessment. Recognize your every lifestyle idiosyncrasy. Evaluate your needs carefully and honestly. The process is guided by the order of construction. You do not want to complete one phase of the project only to return to or damage it when a following phase begins because of an afterthought. Details that you should consider are numerous, and sometimes, important details go overlooked.

THE INTERIOR OF THIS FRENCH DIRECTOIRE SECRETAIRE WAS DISCREETLY REDESIGNED TO HOUSE AUDIO/VIDEO EQUIPMENT, THUS MAINTAINING THE SPIRIT OF THE HOUSE AT LARGE.

Anticipate how things will fit as you begin collecting your home. Before ordering furniture, for instance, verify that the pieces will fit through your doors, in the elevator, and up the staircase. When making a furniture plan, review all the dimensions of the pieces you are considering, and do not forget about traffic patterns. How will you travel from the garage to the kitchen with bags of groceries? What surfaces will you cross at these entry points? Will they be slippery or prone to dirt? Once you open the door with arms full of groceries, where will you put your keys? How will you turn on the lights from a lower garage to light the path to your kitchen? Are you more prone to buy fresh produce than frozen? Maybe you need less freezer capacity. How much cooking will you do, and does this require large pots or platter storage? Where will you most likely sit for coffee to gather yourself for the upcoming workday? Based on your habits, where would you want to locate waste to simplify the separation of recyclables? Where should your laundry room be located for ease of use? Should there be a secondary laundry? Do you need an electronic door entry so you can buzz visitors in? Do you want a discreet security camera at the entry door, dimmers on exterior lighting? These are just a "toe in the water" of the things of life to consider so your house will work in optimal fashion.

AS THE PLAN FOR THIS DRESSING
ROOM EVOLVED, A DRESSING TABLE
HAD TO BE NAVIGATED INTO THE
SPACE. AN ANTIQUE FORM SERVED
BOTH INTEREST AND FUNCTION.

ABOVE: A DAYBED IS A GRACEFUL OPTION IN A GUEST ROOM THAT ALSO SERVES AS A STUDY.

OPPOSITE: THE FURNITURE IN THIS HOME OFFICE IS CONSISTENT WITH THE MODERN AESTHETIC OF THE HOME AT LARGE. A LEDGE FOR CHILDREN'S ART KEEPS THE SPACE LIGHTHEARTED.

MULTIFUNCTIONAL SPACES

While planning, think about which spaces might be able to serve multiple functions too. A home office does not need to be a dedicated room. A guest bedroom may serve this purpose if you integrate a cleverly retooled and attractive furniture piece. Given the ever-shrinking size of laptops, a small desk in a guest room may both serve your need for a work space and benefit the occasional guest. If you purchase a vintage desk, you may consider reinventing it by converting the long shallow drawer so it slides out to hold a keyboard. Or consider transforming an armoire into a workstation. An armoire can be retrofitted so that existing doors pocket inward. That way, when the doors are open, they won't encroach on the room's circulation.

Built-in bookshelves are another option that can be designed to accommodate all the needs of an office. They can also redefine a space in the best possible way, adding interest to a room while serving multiple functions when there is not enough space to fit separate furniture pieces. For instance, you might have a pull-out shelf extend from a bookcase to provide a work surface.

Dining rooms are often one of the most pleasing rooms in the home, but they are typically underused, predominantly for special occasions in many homes. Consider lining the perimeter of your dining room with bookshelves. Place a hardy primitive table at the room's center rather than a precious table that precludes regular use. You may also want to locate outlets beneath the table to accommodate task lighting at the table's center and nonwireless technologies.

A WORKING
LIBRARY CAN
BE ELEGANTLY
APPOINTED
WHILE SERVING
ALL NECESSARY
FUNCTIONS.

REEXAMINE IDEAS

Collecting a home is an investment, so it is not unusual to second-guess earlier decisions. Ruminate over most design decisions carefully, as they will all impact one another in the final outcome; it is far better to make a theoretical mistake in the planning stage than to manage it after a hammer has been wielded. That said, generally I have discovered that often a first instinct is the correct instinct. If, during your effort to bring order to the process, you continue to revisit something time and time again, this uncertainty is telling you to reexamine your decision. If you have forgone something that continues to recur on your wish list, it is perhaps more important than you may want to recognize. This lost opportunity may be forever regrettable once the process has been completed. If budget is an issue, it may be better to wait to do something the way you really want to. Or perhaps you should reprioritize to accommodate that one indulgence.

One of my clients aptly calls this "amortization": spend more on principal objects and less on others. Maybe the cost-efficient option in a powder room is a historic-print wallpaper rather than slabs of marble. Maybe the extravagant faucets should be placed only in the bathrooms where you are most likely to experience them. The home should be oriented toward your personal use and enjoyment.

ARCH-TOP FRENCH DOORS ALLOW THE MORNING LIGHT TO FLOOD INTO THIS MUSIC ROOM. THE CORNER CHAIRS WERE GROUPED IN A MODERN TÊTE-À-TÊTE. THEY HAVE A SCULPTURAL QUALITY IN THIS ARRANGEMENT, BUT GLIDES ON THE FEET ALLOW THEM TO MOVE ABOUT EASILY SO GUESTS CAN ENGAGE IN CONVERSATION.

I have observed that there is an unerring correlation between the level of professional success of my clients and their tendency toward organization. Every second of their day counts. I encourage you to embark upon your project in this disciplined spirit, too. Your home should be visually appealing, comfortable, and hopefully make your life easier. As you map out your course and consider your options, do not just think about the present; plan for the future. I believe it is better to move once "well" than several times, like so many others I know who continue to relocate every three years in their quest to find the perfect home.

LEFT: AN IRON GARDEN TABLE WAS REPURPOSED AS A BASE FOR THE VANITY IN THIS POWDER ROOM.

OPPOSITE: A SHALLOW CABINET WAS DESIGNED TO HOUSE A SENTIMENTAL COLLECTION OF PINK DEPRESSION GLASS. THE COLOR OF THE GLASS INFLUENCED THE SELECTION OF DUSTY ROSE TONES FOR THE CHAIR AND SETTEE.

THESE HANDSOME ANTIQUE PIVOTING HOOKS HAVE SAVED ME UNKNOWN AMOUNTS OF TIME SEARCHING FOR MY KEYS. THEY MAY WELL BE ONE OF MY FAVORITE THINGS IN MY HOUSE.

SELF-EVALUATE

My present Beaux Arts townhouse in Washington, DC, is instructive. I had to carefully plan how I would live in this space. I was moving from a roomy one-floor apartment into a much larger vertical house. Several aspects of the envelope of the house are noteworthy. My new home was originally a single-family residence, but when it was turned into the former Chancery of Oman, it had been carved into a warren of rooms intended to support its "official" use. Multiple offices occupied once-grand spaces. Beneath this labyrinth was a very civilized, well-proportioned, handsome house, and, fortunately, its face-lift was for the most part superficial. Above the drop acoustical ceilings were the original ceilings retaining the original crowns, rosettes, and coffers (although some were in such bad condition that they needed to be replaced). The remnants of the house told me what the intentions for the original building were. Luckily, the house was structurally solid.

Among the seemingly unending decisions that a house brings, particularly when compared with an apartment, is most obviously how to treat multiple floors—in this instance, five. So the first question I asked was where I would spend the majority of my time most comfortably in this new setting. It became apparent that I would have to carve out an interior "dwelling" for myself so the house would perform with the same efficiencies as my former apartment. As I studied the plans, my immediate inclination was to dedicate one floor—the third floor—to my "true" living quarters.

THE HUNT TABLE
WITH FOLDING
EXTENSIONS AND
THE ANTIQUE
ARTICULATING
PORTER'S
CHAIR PROVIDE
A STRIKING
SILHOUETTE IN
FRONT OF THE
FIREPLACE IN
MY BEDROOM.

I planned this space so it would have everything I needed once I settled in for the evening and so I would not have to go up and down the stairs to replenish things. My master bedroom includes a fireplace, and the adjacent sitting room holds a pair of sofas I designed to suit my height for reclining to watch television. There is a concealed built-in refrigerator, a shower and water closet, a laundry room, and a gym that overlooks Rock Creek Park. My dressing room accommodates two antique bathtubs and a few refined furniture pieces. A handsome secretary, which I purchased for my living room, landed here instead because I have such an appreciation for this piece that I wanted it to be placed where I would enjoy it every day.

Many of my most beloved objects have wound up here, where they can be enjoyed most often. I find nothing more comforting than coming back to this space after extended travel. As it turns out, the secretary with all its drawers, compartments, and cubbies supports orderly storage for all things so often lost, such as keys, glasses, cell phones, iPods, adapters, cuff links, and gloves. I am so often on the run that things can easily be misplaced, so the secretary beckons me to instantly clear my pockets with an easily managed discipline, and return things to the familiar and intended places.

ABOVE: THOUGH I WAS ORIGINALLY DRAWN TO THE 1720 ENGLISH BURLED WALNUT SECRETARY FOR AESTHETIC REASONS, IT HAS PROVED TO HAVE IMPORTANT UTILITY; SOMETIMES BEING SELF-INDULGENT IS NOT A BAD THING.

OPPOSITE: YES, I AM OCD, BUT ONLY BECAUSE I LOSE THINGS. WITH THE ORGANIZATION THIS BEAUTIFULLY CRAFTED ANTIQUE SECRETARY OFFERS, I CAN FIND THINGS.

RIGHT: A DINING ROOM SIDEBOARD
WAS CUT DOWN, STRIPPED TO ITS RAW
VENEER, AND REPURPOSED AS A VANITY.

BELOW: KEEPING MY HOUSE ORDERLY
MAKES ME MORE EFFICIENT.

In this same space, the vanity was a dining sideboard in its former life. The original veneer was sanded off and left bare. I used the original wood top to make the template for a limestone replacement that better suited its new utility as a vanity with a sink. A residual benefit of the final floor plan is that it is so functional. No matter how bad my jet lag, I am compelled to unpack and take clothes out of my bags and throw them directly into the nearby wash. This kind of order in my life is essential.

suggestions for storage

As you plan to renovate your existing home or to buy or build a new home, here are some thoughts to capitalize on storage, of which you can never have too much:

- Consider how frequently you use items. This can help determine your storage needs and placement concerns. If you use an item once a year, it can logically be stored in a less accessible area than an item that you use once a week.

- Is space in a mudroom needed for more than coats and hats? Will you need to store sports equipment such as hockey bags, golf clubs, bicycles, or skis?

- Consider having a dedicated location for mail, keys, and bags.

- Exploit cavities under stairs for storage.

Consider how you will use your closet or dressing room:

- Do you prefer your clothes folded in drawers or hanging in a closet?

- Do you want to be able to see all of your clothes at once or do you prefer to conceal clothing behind doors?

- Will you move clothes seasonally?

- Where will you store shoes?

- Will you need a concealed step stool or perhaps a rolling library stair that can travel the room's perimeter on a graceful track to reach upper shelves?

- Do you need easy access to your suitcases?

- Do you want an easily accessible iron and ironing board, a full-length or three-way mirror?

- Consider mounting rod heights based on your actual pant/dress lengths instead of the standard heights.

- Do you hang pants on a clip hanger or fold them over the hanger? The answer will dictate how much long hanging space you will need.

- If you would like a safe, the size of the safe unit raises the question of whether additional structural support is needed. Because large safes can be very heavy, determining the placement and any structural needs ahead of time is important.

4

ENHANCE

REFINE WITH ARCHITECTURAL ELEMENTS

In collecting your home, remember that every detail matters, from the monumental, such as removing walls or adding fireplaces, to the more specific, such as the selection of the handrail and supporting pickets for your central stairs. With the proper balance of vision and discipline, the various decisions you make can all coalesce into something extraordinary.

In this chapter, I will share my thoughts about the many ways that architectural details may significantly enhance an otherwise ordinary interior. I will also share from my own experience how to integrate architectural finds into the home to create a sense of authenticity, character, and a welcoming ambience.

IN THIS GENEROUSLY PROPORTIONED SPACE,
THE ARCHITECTURE DEFINES SEPARATE
SEATING AREAS THAT SUIT BOTH INTIMATE
AND LARGER GATHERINGS.

My penchant for architecture greatly influences my approach to design. I believe the decoration of a house is less important than an intelligently executed foundation—the so-called envelope. Without integration between architecture and interior design, a project will not reach its full potential. The most successful commissions occur when the architect and the decorator are able to bring their different skill sets to the equation from the start. Introducing the decorator later in the project could cause architectural changes specific to the interior decoration that may not have been anticipated. This will add time and expense to your project.

Confident architects welcome opinions in the interest of the greater good. It is important that you feel comfortable expressing yourself under an architect's care so that the evolving plans suit your needs and expectations for how you want to go about collecting your home. Choose an architect you feel will also be open to these ideas, as well as to those of other professionals who may be introduced into the project and who may bring a heightened expertise.

For your part, there should be corresponding deference to the architect with regard to how the project should be built, the cost implications that a change may incur, and, of course, the impact changes may have on the completion deadline. Once your plans are settled, leave the implementation to the architect and general contractor. The task, for all team members, is to honor the project. I may fancy myself to have the heart of an architect, but I am the first to recognize that a vision can only be brought to life under the capable hands of this professional.

GOOD ARCHITECTURE NEEDS LITTLE EMBELLISHMENT. THE STAIR IS SCULPTURE UNDER THE CARE OF FRANCK & LOHSEN ARCHITECTS.

FRENCH DOORS
AND FOLDING
GLASS DOORS
ABOVE THE
COUNTER BRING
INTIMACY TO A
LARGE KITCHEN.

ENVISION POSSIBILITIES

If you are building, renovating, or perhaps just out to enhance the sense of proportion in a room, there are many possible solutions. Walls may be moved. Windows may be enlarged. French doors may be added to create a greater sense of intimacy within a larger space. The character of a room can change significantly by the simple introduction of ceiling treatments, including beams, coffers, ogee molding, skylights, and laylights. And certain window treatments can transform the experience of a room. Shutters, for instance, may enhance the architecture in a room far more than other superficial window coverings.

When thinking about your home, try to view a room almost as if it were a skeletal infrastructure, where the floors, walls, and ceilings interact with one another almost anatomically. All these surfaces should be treated with the same deference to ensure that they work together seamlessly. Remember, form follows function. Windows, for example, may initially seem to call for window treatments. But such treatments may actually be unnecessary if you have privacy and do not need window coverings. Perhaps natural light washing over the room would be more pleasing than gratuitously covering windows simply for the sake of embellishment. In this regard, discreet architectural gestures may be more impactful than ornamental decoration such as a swag or jabot.

If you do want window treatments, however, consider the amount of space required to mount shades or drapery panels. This may help guide which style of window treatment you select. Think about the weight of the window treatments to determine if blocking (wood tied to the wall structure) is necessary to support them. You may want to build cavities for shades or drapery panels to manually or electronically recess into. These can be incorporated behind the crown molding or built into the ceiling. Both may require structural engineering by your contractor and appropriate tradespeople.

Given the costs of window treatments, you also may find that simple ceiling treatments, such as wooden beams, coffers, or beadboard detail, may be far less expensive and may contribute far more to the finished sense of the house. All aspects of the project should be informed by the home's spirit and location. In a country cottage, for instance, you would be more prone to expect timber beams, whereas in an urban townhouse, heavily milled moldings may be more appropriate. On this same note, blatant gestures that are not consistent with the overall character of the house will feel artificial. Bare walls should be treated with this same sensitivity. Treatments may vary from floor-to-ceiling planks to three-quarter-height wainscot.

TAKE IT SLOW

Be forgiving when it comes to retaining elements with history. There is nothing offending about a rough, scratched floor that has been walked upon for ages. This, after all, is what flooring material is intended for. I always gravitate toward things that have a natural patina, because they introduce character and a sense

RECLAIMED WAINSCOT IN MY KITCHEN
ADDS AN ARTISANAL QUALITY TO THE
BUSIEST ROOM OF THE HOUSE.

of history. When I found wainscot in a reclamation warehouse for my home, I did not feel the need to restore it before integrating it into my present kitchen. It was perfect as it was. I was anxious, though, as each width was pulled from its transitional skids. I wondered if there would be enough. Based on the shopkeeper's math, there was not enough. Based on mine, however, there was. I did not care that the mill pattern did not perfectly intersect at each corner of the room.

Interestingly, the only people who have ever commented on this rudimentary, if not sacrilegious, treatment of the wainscot have been architects who were my occasional social guests. Surprisingly, they embrace it, probably as a relief from the exacting requirements typically imposed upon them. Resist the impulse to perfect what is perhaps already perfect; embrace signs of wear and use. In this spirit, you will not be shocked when the eventual incidents of "life" happen.

THE HUNT

When you are beginning your search for great elements for the envelope, I highly encourage a trip to an architectural salvage yard that specializes in reclamation. Here you will find all manner of bygone materials, from antique floors to wall embellishments that have been rescued from prior venues, ranging from antebellum houses to post-and-beam barns.

SOME OF THE ARCHITECTURAL ELEMENTS IN THIS ROOM INCLUDE THE WAINSCOT, WHICH WAS PAINTED WHITE, AND AN ANTIQUE MANTEL FOUND IN LONDON. THIS HOUSE IS CRAFTED IN SUCH A WAY THAT THERE IS NO EVIDENCE IT WAS NOT BUILT DECADES AGO.

THIS PROJECT WAS DRIVEN BY TEXTURAL CHOICES. THE RUSTIC BEAMS, FOUND IN AN ARCHITECTURAL SALVAGE YARD, BRING TEXTURE INTO THIS FAMILY ROOM AND CAMOUFLAGE A TELEVISION AND STORAGE.

These salvage environments charm me, as we live in an era of so many new things made to look old. Architectural reclamation is recycling at its finest. The good people who work in these settings are the stewards of history. These individuals are informally encyclopedic in their reverence for the past, sharing where and how each reclaimed plank was crafted and how challenging it was to preserve during the deconstruction, all of which is utterly heroic and fascinating. These "one-off" time capsules will not be found in ready supply much longer, so be sure and place them in the hands of the craftspeople and tradesmen who will lovingly install them. I have found that true craftspeople embrace these readaptive installations as an uncommon challenge that speaks to their innate talent. A favorite commission for me is one that honors both the craft of the past and the innovation of the present.

One such commission occurred when a family wanted a modern interior that would be respectful of their early-twentieth-century house. The kitchen and the family room were to be part of an addition to the home. Our mandate was to bridge the old and new parts of the house. To this end, naturally, one of our first outings was to a reclamation yard in the distant Virginia countryside. Our day trip with the general contractor turned out to be a summit of sorts. He too had great affection for all things historic and reclaimed.

We examined stack upon stack of timber in search of just the right character and quality. It was a cool fall day that fell on the heels of a torrential rainfall, so, in the true spirit of the settlers, we had to traverse all manner of holes and puddles. We trekked through the fields of surrounding timber inventory, much of it destined to become recycled hardwood flooring or ceiling beams. In the

THE EMBEDDED TIMBER AT THE
WINDOWSILL IS A DISCREET REFERENCE
TO THE HOME'S EXTERIOR. THE PENDANT
IS A PIECE FROM MY COLLECTION WITH
THE URBAN ELECTRIC COMPANY.

end, we were able to piece together the necessary lengths to cover the span of the room where beams would be situated. Some of the timbers had hundred-year-old rusty straps attached, which we left wherever possible once they were finally installed. Since they were used on the ceiling and were out of harm's way, they didn't present any danger, yet these old metal details speak of authenticity.

As a team, we discussed how the timber would relate and append to the ceiling. Thank goodness I was working with a general contractor who was fully on board. Some of the beams that ultimately landed in the house still have carved teenage graffiti from their former lives. These details lend uncompromised character to the home. One can only imagine that these nails were driven into posts in some earlier working farm building. The tendency of some would have been to remove these vestiges. Luckily, this client embraced each timber's historical tale. What looks too weathered for most tastes signals perfection to me.

On this same pilgrimage, we also found reclaimed wood timber that would be used for shelving, windowsills, and an embedded family room fireplace mantel. In each case, the material was then cut and precisely sized so that it appeared to be authentically embedded into the infrastructure, as if from the interior of the original house. The walls here were treated with as much care; a subtle mottling on the surface created an appropriate sense of age and wear. In the end, this project embraced the organically modern sensibility that we had so sought. The contrast between the old and new materials provided an appealing balance without departing from the original house.

AS IN THE
ADJACENT FAMILY
ROOM, THE BEAMS
AND WINDOWSILL
ARE RECLAIMED
TIMBER. THE
APPLIANCES ARE
CLEVERLY AND
CONVENIENTLY
CONCEALED
BEHIND DOORS
IN FUNCTIONAL
COMPARTMENTS.

5

DESIGN

PUT IDEAS INTO ACTION

Now that you have considered the needs of your home, we will get down to some specific applications. Should you add or remove a wall? Should you tailor a space for yourself or perhaps focus more on resale? What might you do to improve doors, millwork, and ceilings? Would it make sense to add a fireplace? We'll explore these subjects in this chapter. These changes are always best in the hands of a qualified professional, but the more informed you are, the more efficient the process will be.

THE WALL WAS ADDED TO FORMALIZE
THE ENTRY FOYER. THE OPENING HOUSES
POCKET DOORS THAT ALLOW THE PRIVATE
ROOMS OF THE HOUSE TO BE CLOSED OFF.

ADDING WALLS

The general instinct is that removing walls opens up a space. In some cases things are better approached counterintuitively: sometimes adding walls may improve a space on both a visual and a functional level. If you aren't using the entire space within a room, you may find that partitioning the unused area with walls or other barriers, such as a sliding art screen or a reclaimed barn door, will allow you to carve out an additional room. Such partitioning may seem counterintuitive because the "open floor plan" has become so prevalent. However, I frequently find great design opportunities by resurrecting walls where they might have been in a former incarnation of the home.

Think about the function that a space is supposed to serve, and make sure it is large enough for that purpose, but not in excess. You might find that you have more space in your home than you originally thought. For example, a large kitchen may accommodate a breakfast area when separated by a wall or French doors. If so, then your breakfast alcove becomes a destination in and of itself. The same is often true of large master suites and open-concept living and dining rooms. You may have a sunroom or an office hiding within another room, which could be an alternative to an invasive addition.

Some spaces beg to be defined. One of my favorite projects illustrates this point. The exterior of this particular home, a 1990s colonial revival, was credible, but the interior was at odds with the traditional character of the house. The first thing I noticed upon entering the house was that it had no formal foyer. The entry gave way to several of the living spaces. The solution was to add a wall that created a formal entry. In this instance, the wall afforded the opportunity of placing a pair of pocket doors that would open into a secondary inner foyer. Adding this wall allowed the family to welcome larger gatherings in the two foyers if need be or to close the pocket doors and create a more intimate foyer for smaller groups.

I WAS DELIGHTED TO DISCOVER THAT MY CLIENT SHARED
A REVERENCE FOR WING CHAIRS. I HAVE ALWAYS FELT
THAT THEIR FORMS HAVE A PARTICULAR VOICE.

REMOVING WALLS

The opposite principle is that opening up walls and simply suggesting the delineation of rooms with architectural elements can help a small space feel larger and residually enhance the flow of natural light through your home. Be careful not to allow open spaces to overwhelm each other, though. Milled columns or sliding doors can delineate spaces while still keeping things open when you want or need them to be.

I recall a center hall apartment that had two parlors and a second bedroom all in tandem. The initial plan was to convert one parlor into the dining room, the center parlor into the living room, and the bedroom into an elegant study. Given the turn-of-the-century architecture and the formality of the space, the plan was to double the size of the original door openings that connected the spaces by adding two sets of double French doors directly across from each other. Because the building was antiquated, new walls were needed to support the weight of the new French doors, so the existing interior walls would have to come down.

The old walls came down during demolition, and during the interim, before the new walls went up, I visited the jobsite. Three windows in the exterior walls provided a sense of light that could not have been fully appreciated before. The effect was transformative: it was clear that the walls should be left down and the French door concept abandoned. Four columns would simply define the space of the two parlors, which now have the benefit of a dramatically improved vista and light. Occasionally, there are moments in a project when a home will actually express itself. Be careful to listen. Sometimes a change of path may be an opportunity to tremendously improve a space; embrace it.

THE OPPOSING COLUMNS STAND WHERE FULL-HEIGHT
WALLS ONCE STOOD. THE WALLS WERE GOING TO BE
REPLACED BY STRONGER WALLS THAT COULD SUPPORT
DOUBLE FRENCH DOORS. BUT WHEN THE WALLS CAME
DOWN, BEAUTIFUL LIGHT CAME IN.

THE COLUMNS MARK
THE LOCATION WHERE
A WALL WITH FRENCH
DOORS WAS INTENDED.
DEMOLITION LED TO
THE DISCOVERY THAT
THE SPACE WAS BETTER
OPEN—A VERY HAPPY
ACCIDENT.

TAILORING YOUR HOME TO YOUR NEEDS

At times, you may be faced with a choice between present comfort and the practicality of future resale value. Perhaps, in terms of resale, it would have been better not to have eliminated that second bedroom in the apartment described above. The owner based his decision on how he wanted to live in the space and the fact that he intended to live there for the long-term. If his commitment to living in the apartment had not been long-term, his decision might have been different.

My former apartment was five thousand square feet. Surely I could have carved out a guest room, but then that would have encouraged guests. There was a demure sleep sofa in the study, but I never let on about this. When I took on a like-minded client, I shared this clandestine guest-avoidance strategy with him. His second bedroom was far more useful as an open study flanked by floor-to-ceiling bookcases. Liberating this space from its formality by lining it with bookshelves was much more consistent with this client's lifestyle—the former bedroom now functions as a large drawing room. All his cherished books (including some that he had written) would be easily reached here. This study also became the perfect resting place for his antique piano and a Louis XVI–style desk, where he could work, as he often does between business trips.

THE SHOWER IN A POWDER ROOM IS CLEVERLY SEQUESTERED BEHIND A SLIDING PANELED DOOR AND OPENED ONLY WHEN NEEDED BY GUESTS STAYING IN A NEARBY BEDROOM.

We approached the eaves of his 1940s cottage in Pennsylvania in this same spirit. Before he bought it, the uppermost floor, an attic, had been divided into several small rooms of varying angled ceiling heights based on the roofline. None of these rooms would accommodate this former decathlete's height. The architect and construction team on the project urged me to take down the walls and open up the space. They were right. Three walls were demolished. A knee wall, which is a low, almost half wall, would serve in lieu of the former stair railing. The openness wholly redefined the space and added visual appeal. Timber beams were embedded in many angles to articulate the ceiling. Where the view from the homeowner's desk was once constrained by rectilinear windows, three large windows, the middle one with an arched top, now take full advantage of the river view. We also gained accidental sleeping niches for feather beds for his young nieces and nephews in odd corners of this open space.

FOR THE GOOD OF THE WHOLE

Generally, I try to preserve any historical elements by restoring or repurposing them. However, there is an exception to every rule. In one particular instance, my client's apartment building had been reconfigured over the years so that what was once a common hallway with an intricate stone pattern and elaborate border detail had been annexed into the newer entry hall of my client's private apartment. After being bisected by the later common hallway wall, the octagonal tiles, in a white and red floral mosaic, had lost their earlier context. Because the original tile pattern now within my client's apartment had been compromised, this was an instance where it could reasonably be removed.

AN ATTIC SPACE THAT COMMANDED
RIVER VIEWS WAS REDESIGNED TO
ACCOMMODATE THIS WORK SPACE.

The entry hall to this apartment was perhaps the most relevant space in the apartment—it had perfectly grand proportions, high ceilings, deep original plaster cove moldings, and the most gracious sensibility. It was, in effect, the spine of the apartment, and an enviable one indeed. An entry of this scale, which makes a perfect gallery, is a bygone blessing seldom seen these days. The foyer hall gave way to the rest of the rooms in the apartment, the three spaces—the dining room, living room, and study—among them. In this instance, uniformly treated floors would greatly improve the unfolding experience of the apartment at large. After I discussed this idea with my client, he agreed that replacing the tile with hardwood was in the best interest of the renovation.

STAIR AS ART

On another project, just the opposite action came into play. Rather than remove an original architectural element (which I rarely do anyway), I worked hard to save it. My client had bought a country property where a series of renovations that predated his acquisition were, shall we say, "better ideas at the time." You could almost precisely date the renovations to their moment by the materials used, most glaringly the metal spiral staircase that accessed the third floor. Placing a new stair here was challenging because of the very limited footprint. The innovation of spiral stairs is the small space they require.

The issue here was that the style of the stair was such an obvious departure from the original fabric of the house, a quaint cottage. The original materials were by and large charming, rough hewn, and artisanal. With its industrial, manufactured character, however, the spiral stair felt foreign in this setting.

A STAIRCASE DISTILLED TO ITS SIMPLEST
FORM WAS CREATED IN COLLABORATION
WITH SULLIVAN BUILDING & DESIGN GROUP.

THE PARTITION
CABINETS WERE
ADDED TO
PROVIDE A MORE
INTIMATE EATING
SPACE WITHIN
THE OTHERWISE
OPEN KITCHEN
PLAN. THE
CHAIRS IN THE
KITCHEN WERE
REPLICATED AS
BAR STOOLS AT
THE KITCHEN
ISLAND.

During a local shopping trip, I noticed a primitive spiral stair that was relegated to the corner of an antiques warehouse. It had been reclaimed from an older structure, probably a house. The stair featured triangular treads. The underside was exposed so you saw the structure of the treads and risers. My client's home had ceiling height limitations and the footprint could not change, so we had to find a solution that would work within these parameters. My fortuitous peripheral glance would finally inspire the new stair for this project. The stair I had come upon was diminutive: the perfect solution stood before me. Dwarfed by the size of the warehouse, it may not have otherwise stood out but for this particular location, and had it been snugged in its original setting, I would not have been able to view its underside.

Once the former stair in the cottage was removed, the demolition revealed the surrounding infrastructure of the supporting walls. The composition of the interior infrastructure beneath the drywall was a relatively open wire mesh and plaster; an intriguing craft of construction and an extraordinary gift of texture to the project. The original infrastructure, when exposed, creates a time capsule of sorts, and the replacement spiral stair structure consists of old timber. The result serves both as a stair and as an abstract sculpture. Somehow, this integration of materials is appropriate to the cottage. The modern design, because of its composition of rough-hewn timber, honors the original character of the house. The stair is informed by history while looking forward to the future. Remember, an open dialogue and a willingness to take chances can lead to the discovery of far greater solutions than can a singular vision.

DOORS, MILLWORK, AND BUILT-INS

Sometimes, I use doors as walls. I like rooms to serve multiple functions. Often large spaces, perhaps in need of intimacy, inspire my approach, which is to create a gathering place within the existing boundaries. The need for smaller, more intimate areas is most often found in the kitchen, with its ubiquitous sprawling integrated eating space. Kitchens are the heart of most houses; thus they have taken on adjunct uses. I generally encourage creating a seating alcove of some sort—for example, through the addition of a wall that separates the kitchen proper from an interior "eating" area. French or glass pocket doors often work beautifully for this purpose. This way the kitchen can both facilitate the cooking and serving but also stand separate for intimate dining. I designed the kitchen in my townhouse with French doors to create a sunroom/breakfast room. There is nothing like taking part in the making of a meal, then getting to enjoy it without worrying that the kitchen exploded in a mess during the cooking. Save the dishes for later, and enjoy your guests.

The addition of doors to a room allows you the option to shut down the space or to open it up for larger gatherings. When you are deciding whether to add doors, consider realistically how much entertaining you will do, and the number of guests you would host. If you have a small family that does not entertain formally, you may not need a way of creating pockets of activity, but you might still enjoy the big "reveal" on holidays or other special occasions that opening the doors into a room, especially a dining room, allows.

Evaluate whether it would be worth it to replace any of the doors in your home. I once found a pair of massive antique doors in a reclamation warehouse in Palm Beach, Florida, that were perfect for the existing architectural conditions of a client's house. They complemented the scale, sense of place, and vocabulary of the home. I had the vintage doors finished with a matte black paint.

HERE THE RECLAIMED
DOORS CONCEAL A
CAVITY THAT ONCE
HOUSED A LOWER
CABINET WITH A
MIRROR ABOVE. THE
PREVIOUS TREATMENT
DID NOT SUIT THE
FORMALITY OF THE
MAIN ENTRANCE.
THESE HEAVY
ITALIANATE DOORS
SALVAGED FROM AN
ADDISON MIZNER
BUILDING ARE
MORE APPROPRIATE
TO THE GRAVITY
OF THE EXISTING
ARCHITECTURE.

FIREPLACES

If the option exists for a fireplace, it can be one of the most pleasant features in a room. Given the available offerings, these do not have to be architecturally invasive, as they were in the past. Fireplaces can now be introduced into an existing area without masonry walls. To me, nothing is more engaging than a fireplace, even in an outdoor setting.

In one weekend house, the living room possessed an extraordinary view of the river, but it didn't have a fireplace. I could imagine this room as the seasons changed, and I thought of how irresistible it would be to view the distant frozen river while being warmed beside a blazing, crackling fire. This image was later reinforced when, prior to construction, my client and I went to a nearby nineteenth-century inn for dinner. There, opposite our table, on a rainy winter's eve, was the most enchanting walk-in fireplace. Once upon a time, this was indeed how homes were heated. Though the existing conditions in my client's house precluded a masonry fireplace, I designed a gas fireplace to suggest masonry, which would complete the atmosphere in this living room.

The walk-in fireplace reference was far too lofty for our stonemason's taste, and he was right. He suggested pargeting, a plasterlike application with a mortar consistency. Pargeting can be accomplished in several different ways and was traditionally applied to brick walls as a means of inexpensive repairs. It looks as if you have applied grout over the entire brick wall. It can also be painted, allowing you to achieve an unobtrusive finish with a subtle suggestion of added texture.

THE FIREPLACE WAS THOUGHTFULLY
DESIGNED SO THAT ITS ADDITION
WOULD BE CONSISTENT WITH THE
VOCABULARY OF THE HOME.

ABOVE: THE HEAVILY CARVED ANTIQUE
MANTEL REDEFINED THE CHARACTER
OF THIS MASTER BEDROOM.

OPPOSITE: THE RECLAIMED MANTEL
FIT THE SPIRIT OF THE HOUSE; THE
PATINATED METAL GRATE CONCEALS
A GAS FIREPLACE.

Because it is a hand-troweled finish that differs depending on the mason's particular technique, knowing your craftspeople and working with them to develop and review finish samples is key to being sure you achieve the final expected outcome. I knew pargeting would work here with the native architecture, so I deferred to the stonemason's wisdom. Using local craftspeople whenever possible in a historic setting is always a smart choice. The resulting fireplace brings this room and its surroundings into perfect harmony.

In another setting, I had an antique French iron fireplace grate (with its original small doors, their intricate filigree still intact) retrofitted to attach to the glass-front gas fireplace insert in the living room. This execution suited the living room while allowing visitors to view the fire's movement through the antique grate. The glass fireplace insert would have otherwise defeated the sense and integrity of the new interior. Always strive for consistency of craft and materials.

The master bedroom in this same project took on a grander presence when we replaced a new mantel with a far more diminutive antique carved marble mantel. This elegant architectural element greatly enhanced the room's scale and sense of character.

CEILINGS

The ceiling often goes overlooked and untouched, but a ceiling treatment can greatly affect the entire sense of the room. A gestural shallow coffer in the ceiling can lend subtle interest. It may seem that adding a treatment to an already low ceiling may visually lower it, but a deeply punctuated embellishment can actually create a greater sense of height. In this instance, the recesses created by the existing ceiling may suggest that the original ceiling was far higher. If you paint this detail the same as the ceiling, you are in effect simply articulating the ceiling as texture. Even the most basic addition of a reclaimed plaster rosette can surprisingly improve an otherwise sterile ceiling.

EACH FRAGMENT OF THIS ANTIQUE CEILING ROSETTE WAS INSTALLED INDEPENDENTLY. THE LINES AND CRACKS ARE EVIDENCE OF THE PAST LIVES OF THIS RECLAIMED PIECE OF ARCHITECTURE. RESTORATION WOULD HAVE BEEN FAR LESS COMPLICATED.

NATURAL CEILING LIGHT

Skylights of various sorts have long been used to bring light into homes. Laylights are the forebearer to the ubiquitous plastic bubble that has come to be the present standard for skylights. In a Tudor-style home in Washington, DC, architect Donald Lococo designed a stained glass laylight beneath a skylight as a ceiling treatment that would naturally illuminate the formal stair of this home. Donald kindly invited me, as the interior decorator on the project, into the conversation while the laylight was taking shape.

The laylight under his care was very subdued looking, though complex in its design. He prodded me for my opinion about how the glass should be executed. Rather than use stained glass, together with the client we landed on a combination of milk glass of varying opacity. The laylight in this context was not to be a monument, but rather an appropriate way to diffuse light through the stairwell.

When my staff and I approached a Spanish colonial home, the master bedroom provided a great opportunity for a ceiling treatment. The owners wanted to maximize the ceiling height, but the roofline precluded any typical options. The design of a laylight evolved again as a solution. It would have to be divided into two panels that stepped up from one level to the next. The edges of the laylight recess were clad with patinated steel collars, and an asymmetric linear

A MODERN
STEPPED LAYLIGHT
CONCEIVED AS ART
IN THE MASTER
BEDROOM OF THIS
SPANISH COLONIAL
HOME IS VISIBLE
FROM THE STAIR.

grid was created with the panels themselves. In this case, the ceiling treatment performed several functions. It provided additional natural light and a credible cover for artificial lights that could be dimmed until they barely emanated light, and the laylight also served as art.

In one instance, a secondary residence had a number of existing skylights that did not feel true to the original architecture. The kitchen presented the biggest challenge. The homeowner had no plans to replace the existing roof, so we were left to contend with the present structural conditions, which included 1980s modern plate glass skylights in a pitched ceiling. The owner wanted to maintain the light source, so covering them was not an option. The existing mullioned windows throughout the house inspired an obvious and consistent solution. Since the skylight was a deeply recessed cavity, mullioned windows were suspended from chains. These echoed the existing windows, thus honoring the architecture. Likewise, they camouflaged the unattractive 1980s skylights. They also created the visual illusion of leveling the pitched ceiling because they paralleled the floor and the kitchen beams. Each challenge brings new opportunity.

ABOVE: THIS MASTER BEDROOM IS DRIVEN ENTIRELY BY TEXTURE PLAY, FROM THE CONCRETE SHELVING TO THE AFRICAN BARK CLOTH ABOVE THE BED. SUBTLE ILLUMINATION FROM THE LAYLIGHT ABOVE ACCENTUATES THESE CONTRASTING TEXTURES.

OPPOSITE: I DESIGNED THE WINDOWS SUSPENDED ON CHAINS TO FRAME THE EXISTING MODERN SKYLIGHTS ABOVE.

THE DANGLING HOOK AT THE BOTTOM OF MY LIVING ROOM PANELED SHUTTERS IS BOTH FUNCTIONAL AND AESTHETICALLY PLEASING. PLACING THE HOOK LOW ALLOWED ME TO MAINTAIN THE FUNCTION WITHOUT VISUALLY OVERWHELMING THE SPACE.

SHUTTERS

Shutters enhance both the beauty and the privacy of a space. Occasionally, their architectural quality may complement a window where draperies might otherwise diminish the beauty of the window in its architectural context. Shutters may blend into the architecture of a space or be chosen to add a contrasting decorative element that reads as part of the architecture even though they are actually superficial. They also offer a good alternative where fabric is not a practical solution (such as in a kitchen or laundry room) and can be used as a foil to hide the true proportions of a window behind.

I usually prefer paneled shutters to those with louvers. When I do use louvers, I like them to be narrow—historically inspired. Louvered shutters may be used in a space where privacy is important but natural light is still preferred, as in a bathroom or bedroom.

I am particularly partial to shutters that are not full height, but that instead go slightly above the midsection on the window—five-eighths height—to trick the eye so that a window may appear to be full height. If the shutter is installed with this in mind, it can make the window appear longer and more graceful. The rule of thumb is to cover the center sash, so you don't know where it is. In my living room, for example, the shutters go to the floor to further suggest that the windows are full length. This adds height to the room while still allowing natural light in.

Shutters in this execution, combined with Roman shades, are a great way of providing privacy on the lower half of the window and room-darkening features on the upper half. The shutters can be closed but still allow natural light to come in. At night or during a bright day, the shades can be lowered to cover the entire window. Shutters are especially appealing in heavily milled settings such as libraries, where they can discreetly disappear with Harmon hinges, which are recessed, or pocket pivot hinges, in effect folding the shutters into the architecture.

I've used shutters with screens built in to camouflage radiators and heating, ventilating, and air-conditioning units more than once. Finding interior shutters for my living room windows was a bit of an undertaking, as the windows are rather large and I was in search of reclaimed shutters. En route to the airport in North Carolina, I spotted them in a window we were passing at fifty-five miles per hour. Despite my already being late for my flight, this was an instance when brakes needed to be applied. I soon found myself ushering my companions into the store, and so I acquired the weathered shutters I had been in search of in North Carolina by way of a Belgian farmhouse.

FURNITURE INTEGRATED INTO ARCHITECTURE

A furniture piece may be cleverly integrated into the architecture and can provide unexpected benefits. In this spirit, I am always on the hunt for ways to incorporate interesting furniture pieces that will function in efficient ways in various rooms throughout a house. In my kitchen, I formerly had a large pot

ABOVE: A ONCE-FREESTANDING
ÉTAGÈRE WAS MODIFIED TO PROVIDE
SHELVING ON MY KITCHEN ISLAND.

OPPOSITE: IN A DINING ROOM THAT
OFTEN FUNCTIONS AS A WORK
SPACE, THE BAROQUE-STYLE TABLE
LAMPS STAND IN FOR A TYPICAL
CHANDELIER. THE SETTEE BREAKS
UP THE REGIMENT OF CHAIRS
MARCHING AROUND THE TABLE.

rack hanging above the center island. This provided ease of access to larger pots and pans and multiplied much-needed storage. As it turns out, despite its utility, it was too visually chaotic at the room's center for my taste. The solution was already present in the adjacent eating area. I retrofitted an iron étagère to bridge the top of the island and the ceiling. The result significantly improved the sense of intimacy in this large space, anchoring its center while supporting ease of use and open storage. The kitchen now works akin to a commercial kitchen, as the étagère can be used to plate or platter dishes as they are prepared. The pots and pans are stowed away, and instead, my beautiful collection of white ironstone takes pride of place in the open storage.

In another case in which furnishings were used in an innovative and functional way, a pair of Baroque lamps ended up defining a future dining room. This dining room had unusually low ceilings, so lamps at the center of the table would be an innovative way to light the room. While shopping early in the process, I came upon what I thought would be the perfect pair of lamps, but the space presented several challenges. The floor joists that were exposed from the floor above the dining room would not allow for any sort of recessed fixture, as all conduits would be visible. Finally, we designed a long dining table to function both for entertaining and as a secondary work space. Inspired by an Asian altar table, the piece had to be precise in its execution. Holes were bored where the lamps would be placed. The surplus was salvaged so that the table could be functional without lamps in another setting. The placement of the floor outlets was exacting, and the center legs of the table were hollowed to hide the cords from the lamps.

DELICATE
PICKETS AND
HANDRAILS
WERE SELECTED
TO SUPPORT
THE GRACEFUL
STAIRS DESIGNED
BY ARCHITECT
RICHARD CRONE.

INTEGRATE INTERIOR
ARCHITECTURE AND DESIGN

The integration of the lamps into the dining room described earlier underscores the collaboration required among the decorator, the architect, and multiple tradespeople. Another example speaks to this point as well. Often the preliminary set of drawings will have a floor plan that has not evolved, in which all the furniture is placed at the room's perimeter. If the decorator then wants to orient the furniture at the room's center to function comfortably for varying sorts of gatherings, this seemingly inconsequential change might actually require floor outlets at the room's center. Relocating the furniture also frees these walls for art that now may need picture lights and/or overhead directional spotlights.

A bedroom requires similar thoughtfulness. Sconces at bedside ought to be individually controlled from both sides of the bed. This sounds simple enough, but to locate these sconces, you have to contemplate the size of the headboard, the length of the user's arm, the width of the bed, and the height of the mattress. Striving for the simultaneous development of design and architectural features will help you preserve harmony throughout the process and the home and may also help you avoid costly changes later.

ABOVE: OGEE MOLDING IS A FAVORITE.
IT CAN REDEFINE A SPACE WHEN
ADDED TO WALLS, BOOKSHELVES,
AND CROWN MOLDING.

OPPOSITE: A COMPLEX BATHROOM
VANITY THAT BISECTS THE SHOWER
CAVITY SERVES AS A BENCH WITHIN.
THE PENDANT IS A PIECE FROM
MY COLLECTION WITH THE URBAN
ELECTRIC COMPANY.

OGEE

One of the easiest ways of adding interest to a room is with molding on a wall or ceiling. An ogee is an S-shaped piece of molding that has both a convex and a concave curve. Most often used in crown molding, it can be used to add detail or depth to any base mold, door slab, or wall in a variety of executions. Ogee can also be beneficial as a finish detail for prefabricated built-ins. In my dining room, following the historic reference of the home, I used a simple three-quarter-inch ogee as picture mold on the walls to replace the original Greek key pattern. I wanted architectural detail as gestures, not as pronounced features.

HINGES

When an environment is visually spare, it is critical that the envelope be precise, as these settings tend to be unforgiving of any visual clutter. Long after completing one project, I was on the phone with my client, who told me how restful it felt being in her home. She shared, "I don't know what it is about this apartment that makes it feel so serene." I asked her to look around and tell me how many door hinges she could see. She couldn't find any. I had very deliberately hidden all hinges. Often what you don't see is as important as what you do.

It was perhaps this same sensibility that led me to have artists engineer an architectural bathroom vanity that spans the shower's glass partition and becomes a shower bench on the other side. The artisans made it look easy, but it was nothing short of an engineering marvel. God bless every artist I collaborate with; there would be no innovative work without you.

suggestions for bathrooms

When planning your bathroom, there are many options to consider. Before selecting fixtures and fittings, you may want to think about the following:

- Do you have a preference for a soaking tub versus a shower? Will a tub enhance resale?

- Are you hoping to incorporate a heavy bathtub or a heavy stone slab? The structure of older homes may not accommodate the extra weight without reinforcement.

- Is privacy a concern? Consider window placement and whether you would like a separate water closet.

- Where would towel bars and/or hooks be most useful? If you are not installing them directly into the wall studs, blocking may be needed.

- Do you prefer open vanities or is storage more critical? If using an exposed basin, select one that is glazed on the underside for a finished look. The standard may not be glazed.

- Be sure to specify the finish for exposed pipe fittings.

- Would you like a towel warmer? Certain models may have plumbing requirements that need to be anticipated.

- Consider ordering the toilet trip lever in a finish to match other fittings. Having matching finishes supports a harmonious appearance.

- Would you like a steam shower? Consider where the operating system will be housed and where the controls will be located. These are often cumbersome and have very specific requirements, so deciding early in the process is advisable.

- Would you like radiant heating for the floor or shower seat? These can affect electrical and/or plumbing.

- Do you need an electrical outlet in your medicine cabinet or the drawer where you store your hair dryer, electric razor, and so forth?

- Grout joint widths are visually impactful. Some tumbled tiles will have inconsistent grout joints; you may want to request a mock-up sample from the tile vendor to see the finished product.

- Tile and grout color may respond differently in varying light conditions; review the samples in place.

THIS MASTER
BATHROOM IS
A STUDY IN
SERENITY. A
SOAKING TUB
AND CANDLES—
SIMPLE DOES IT.

6

CONNECT

INTEGRATE PAINT AND TEXTILE PALETTES

Paint is what most inspires the spirit and experience of a home. Because of its overwhelming design presence, paint can either tremendously enhance or defeat an environment. Thus the selection of paint is perhaps one of the most important and least costly design decisions to be made. Your paint choices will inform the way textiles and textures relate to harmoniously connect the home. In this chapter, you will find several examples of how to quietly connect color.

A common mistake that I often see is a lack of color cohesion as I walk progressively through a house. The most profound misstep is that the selection of paint is done in a piecemeal fashion—one room at a time instead of with consideration of the house as a whole.

I prefer relatively neutral monochromatic palettes because of how they unify the experience of a house as it unfolds. In developing a color palette for a project, I appreciate subtle distinctions between varying shades of white. We will select a principal color that is intended to connect the house through its common elements. These are its public spaces—hallways, foyers, stairwells, the underside of stairs, and any other spaces throughout the home that are prone to intersect. They are the "spine" of the house. The best example is the stairwell. Stairwells give way to landings that give way to hallways. These areas in the home should be carefully considered, because they are indeed related. These common spaces are also most problematic because they always raise the question, Where should the color end? Generally, unless there is an intervening architectural detail such as wainscot or a chair rail, there is no logical place for the paint to end. Therefore, the most intelligent way to deal with this ever-present challenge is through the use of the same or similar color in all these areas.

Base mold, which separates the wall from the floor, often extends throughout the entire home. For instance, if your living room has a base mold that wraps around to the foyer opening and the living room is painted in a distinctly different color from the foyer, at what point should the living room base mold color stop before it wraps around the wall, or should it wrap continuously into the adjacent foyer? And once in the foyer, what happens at the stair, and so on? This type of flow throughout a home is why I often advocate using colors of similar tonality to gracefully bring harmony to these spaces. This logic holds true no matter what the palette. Whatever the wall color, the base mold and crown mold should respond to the primary color selected. So paint the base a similar color that just slightly differs to articulate the wall from the trim. This distinction can also be achieved by using the same colors in different finishes: matte for the walls, and satin or high gloss on wood trim.

THE FRAMED
PLASTER
CHILDREN'S
HANDPRINTS ARE
THOUGHTFULLY
ENGAGED IN
THIS PALETTE.

Interior doors can also be challenging in terms of creating a cohesive connection. If you have doors to private rooms that are painted one color on the interior side and another color on the exterior side, where should these colors end? When the door is open, you will see its hinged section, so which space should govern your color choice? Similarly when a door is open (generally into a room), you will perhaps experience both colors more often than anticipated in the room's interior. This dilemma may suggest that all doors throughout the home or at least in all areas where they will be viewed together should be painted in the same color. These decisions become far more noticeable in the context of a home that does not have a uniform palette. This is why I strongly encourage studying the house in its entirety before committing to a paint color palette.

EXTERIOR PAINTING

I once worked with a client on a Georgian-style home. The house was beautifully sited on the property, its architecture discreet and its scale unpretentious. The client did not want to impose an addition on the structure, but it did require work to accommodate her family's needs within its existing footprint. The house was older, with mature plantings. The entire east facade was covered in climbing hydrangea. I asked, "Could the hydrangea attached to the side of the house be suspended in such a way that it could be preserved and reattached, given that new windows will be going in? I would hate to see it harmed." She said, "I think the entire exterior of the house should be painted." Nothing better than a clairvoyant client! The house, beautiful though it was, greatly benefitted when the existing pinkish brick was painted white and then power washed so that it appeared to be consistently worn, respectful of the home's age and the character of the neighboring houses. The hydrangea was preserved by an interim scaffolding system that held the plants away from the structure while the new windows were installed and the house was painted.

The point is that the exterior of the house is the first instance where you should begin to consider what the interior will finally feel like. Before you paint, you must first view the house as a whole. Carefully take into account the sense of your home throughout to ensure color continuity. There must be a harmony of color gradation from the outside going inside and from room to room as the house is experienced. The color palette should inform all the future embellishments, from textiles to furniture, art, and other thoughtfully selected objects about the house. Is the house formal, casual, or seasonal? Color choices will respond to these intentions if chosen carefully. Once the sensibility of the home is established, color will guide the decorative vocabulary.

THE COLOR CORE OF THE HOME

The exterior color is only the tip of the iceberg. Once you have contemplated the house in a broader, more philosophical manner, then there are a host of other things to be considered before you make your final selection of colors. As indicated earlier, common areas, hallways, and stairwells are often the most important and the most logical places to begin making color decisions. Though these spaces are often the last considered in the process of selecting the palette, the selection of paints for them is perhaps more critical than that for rooms about the home.

Because common spaces are also generally the most traveled areas, care should be taken in selecting not only the color, but also the finish. How active is your household? Where will there be a need for the most durable paints, and, conversely, where might there be an opportunity for a more precious treatment if this is desirable?

In general, flatter paints tend to be the best at minimizing visible flaws in the underlying wall surface. Glossier paints tend to emphasize imperfections. Flat paint finishes, however, can be less forgiving of superficial marks. In higher traffic areas or hallways, you may want to consider some sort of paneling, an architectural detail that is more durable than drywall, in order to survive being bumped by vacuums and moving luggage, by storing lacrosse sticks, and so on. A glossier, more washable finish that is more forgiving may be the appropriate choice here for paneling or walls. Kitchens and bathrooms, of course, need the most durable paints. Generally, I specify satin finishes for doors, trims, mill-work, crown molding, and paneling detail, as these are usually long-lasting and may also residually enhance the architecture. The slightly different sheen between walls finished with a flat paint and moldings finished in a satin paint allows the architectural details of the moldings to stand out and enhances the architectural effects of these details in the most discreet execution. Be sure to consult a paint expert regarding the best finish to suit your specific needs.

WALL TREATMENTS

Consider durability, humidity (which can affect wallpaper), traffic, and/or util-ity when selecting wall treatments. Certain wall covering materials are not advised in a bathroom, while others may be too delicate to stand up to the heavy traffic in a central hallway.

Another thing to contemplate before selecting your color palette is the vari-ety of wall treatments that may add interest and perhaps benefit acoustics or minimize future maintenance or touch-ups. Paintable textural wallpapers are one such example meant for this very purpose. These alternatives should be explored in advance of paint color selections because they may need to be inte-grated into the treatment or applied to future surfaces. The base treatment may need to be preapplied and may be compatible with only certain paints.

Paintable wallpapers will lend texture to a wall where actively patterned wallpaper may not be desired. Even if you opt for a vivid floral pattern, the

THE SHADOWY MOVEMENT OF THE
VENETIAN PLASTER TREATMENT
HONORS THE ROMANTIC OIL PAINTING
SUSPENDED ON AN ANTIQUE HOOK.

paper's background color should relate to core colors used throughout the house. I cannot caution enough that even papers that appear to have a neutral, if not white, background generally don't look neutral once placed opposite other colors. There is always an undertone, even if it is very subtle. When you are making color choices elsewhere in the home, consider the paper's background tint to ensure consistency. It can become very pronounced in the company of other paints and paper. It is advisable to get true samples of the dye lots available for your wallpaper so that you can be certain they are all compatible.

MOLDINGS

Be sure to consider all intersecting base molding, case molding (which is used to frame doors and windows), and crown molding in the context of both paint and wallpaper. You will not often encounter rooms that do not intersect by way of some continuous molding that follows from the perimeter of one room to the next.

Shoe mold, in particular, is a detail occasionally overlooked, but one worth considering. Shoe molding (which covers any gaps between the base molding and the flooring) can be painted to match trim or stained to match the floors. Specify your preference with your contractor. Shoe mold that is stained is often finished and installed by the hardwood floor vendor. Shoe mold that is painted is usually installed by a carpenter or general contractor, then finished by the painter. This is a conversation worth having in advance.

THE DELICATELY CARVED SIDEBOARD WAS GESSOED AND
PAINTED WITH A COLOR REFERENCING THE WAINSCOT
BEYOND. THIS CHOICE HONORS THE BOLD SUBJECT OF
THE EDWARD FINNEGAN GRAPHITE DRAWING.

SEEING CHOICES IN CONTEXT

Gather all your options together as samples and/or wall strikes (paint colors you test on the wall that you plan to paint) before you commit. It is not uncommon for colors to reflect, respond to, or conflict with one another, which you would not realize when looking at them separately. Always try paint in the settings where you intend to live with it. Even the light where you view a sample will significantly impact its appearance.

Once when I was working on a project remotely, even though the color palette was developed with great precision, it failed once samples were viewed in the intended spaces. A former owner had installed UV-protected glass throughout the property to protect his art. The pale pink tint of the glass was indiscernible except with the intended neutral palette; most of the pale whites selected looked pink in situ. The never-ending joke among my colleagues whenever we assemble a presentation is that white can be be viewed as infinite colors; there is no true white. I get extraordinary good-natured grief about my "hypersensitivity to color." The environments where we work, though filled with subtle hints of color when viewed by colleagues and clients, are often perceived by others to be relatively colorless in their final execution.

CHOOSING COLORS

Once you understand an environment—its architectural opportunities and challenges, the sense of place, the light in the morning, at noon, and at night—and your lifestyle, the rest is up to you and how you choose to collect colors in your home. Colors so affect our daily lives, they should be chosen with care and discipline. These decisions may profoundly affect your mood. Certain shades may make you feel calm or agitated, happy or sad, warm or cool. Be sure to live with paint samples for a sufficient amount of time, at a minimum a day and possibly for a week, in order to truly experience them. Once settled, choose the colors that please you the most.

I have included a few of my favorite colors throughout this chapter in the context of how they work in some rooms that my staff and I have decorated, as well as in Appendix A. Once more, these should always be sampled in place and alongside one another and preferably in concert with all of the textiles, which we will discuss later in this chapter.

TRAINING YOUR EYE: PAINT

I challenge anyone to put five different samples of white on a wall next to one another, look at them, and tell me they are not different colors—one may look pinkish, one may look bluish, and one may look yellowish, even though individually they all looked white. Pay attention to the undertones when you select paints. They need to work in harmony with the fabrics and furnishings throughout your home.

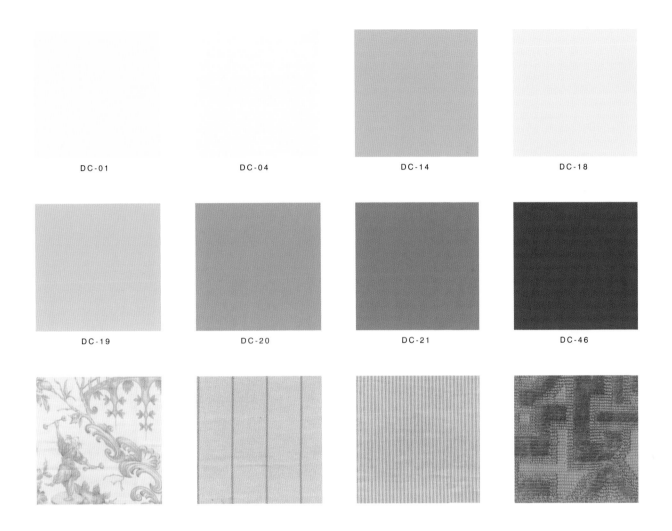

DC-01   DC-04   DC-14   DC-18

DC-19   DC-20   DC-21   DC-46

THE SPIRIT OF THIS HOUSE WAS FORMAL, YET ENGAGING, SO OUR
MISSION WAS TO USE COLOR AND PATTERN TO AMPLIFY THESE
EXISTING CONDITIONS. THE LIVING ROOM HERE EPITOMIZES THESE
CHARACTERISTICS. THE BOOKSHELVES WERE AN ADDITION. THE
FORMER FIREPLACE MANTEL WAS REPLACED WITH A HISTORICAL
MANTEL THAT REFERENCED THE HOME'S ARCHITECTURE. THE
SURROUND WAS CHANGED TO A CALMER GRAY-GREEN SLATE. THIS
STONE WAS SELECTED SO THAT IT WOULD INTEGRATE WITH THE
FUTURE TEXTILE PALETTE, WHICH WAS DERIVED IN TURN FROM THE
MOST FAINT COLOR REFERENCE TO THE AUBUSSON RUG. USING
THE TOILE ON ITS REVERSE DULLED THE MORE GRAPHIC PATTERN
PRECISELY TO THE SUBTLE GREEN PALETTE OF THE ROOM.

DC-37   DC-38

DC-39   DC-40

DC-45   DC-47

THE FORMAL WOOD PANELING IN THIS DINING
ROOM IS PAINTED IN A PALE MUSHROOM HUE. A
DARK WOOD STAIN WOULD HAVE BEEN OPPRESSIVE
IN THIS SETTING. THE WALL ABOVE THE MILLWORK
IS UPHOLSTERED TO LEND A GREATER SENSE OF
INTIMACY TO THE SPACE.

SHOP PAINTED VERSUS FIELD PAINTED

When you're finishing doors or other millwork, be sure to specify paint-grade or stain-grade wood. Paint-grade is often less expensive. Stain-grade wood is of a higher quality than paint-grade. You'll also need to specify whether you want it shop painted or field painted. In terms of aesthetics, shop-painted wood will give you a "factory finish," while field-painted wood will show the hand of the painter. As far as cost goes, field painting can be less expensive, but it depends on the conditions of the site. If you're adding a built-in to an existing room, it may be easier to shop paint it to avoid having to mask off other areas and risk damage. On the other hand, if it's new construction, it may be more efficient to field paint. This may be especially true if there are several built-ins.

PAINTING FURNITURE

Paint has yet another role: it can virtually transform a furniture piece. On more than one occasion, I have had to finesse a family heirloom or a furniture piece brought to a relationship by one partner that he or she was sentimentally attached to when single. At first glance, these pieces often seem inconsistent with the new aesthetic that the couple has established, but this challenge can be overcome and the piece integrated into its new environment with some ingenuity. A "noncommittal brown" piece can often be significantly improved by painting it with black high-gloss paint. Replacing an existing wood top with stone can yield great benefit too. After I transformed an heirloom buffet in this spirit for a client, it turned out so beautifully, it landed very prominently in the dining room.

THE DINING ROOM IS ENCHANTING
AT NIGHTFALL AS THE PALE
BLUE VENETIAN PLASTER WALLS
RADIATE WITH CANDLELIGHT.

DC-05   DC-25   DC-27

DC-26   DC-28   DC-24

THE ARCHITECTURE IN THIS HOUSE IS SO DISCREET AND ORDERED
THAT IT NEEDED TO BE TREATED WITH GREAT SENSITIVITY. THE WALL
COLORS, THOUGH NEUTRAL IN APPEARANCE, HAVE THE FAINTEST HINT
OF BLUE, WHICH BECOMES MORE PRONOUNCED AS YOU PROGRESS
THROUGH THE HOME. THE DISTANT DINING ROOM IS TREATED IN A
PALE BLUE VENETIAN PLASTER.

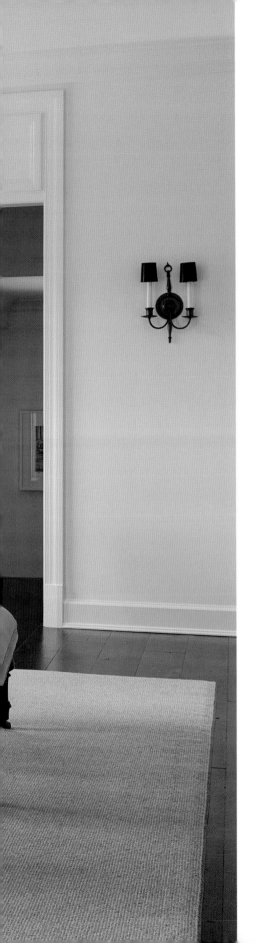

DC-41   DC-42   DC-43

DC-44   DC-15   DC-16

AN UNUSUALLY BROAD SECOND-FLOOR LANDING IS THE PERFECT
VENUE FOR FAMILY RESPITE. THIS PALETTE WAS SELECTED BECAUSE
OF THE CLIENT'S RESPONSE TO ITS WARMTH. ONCE MORE THE GRAY
GREEN IS AN INTERVENING UNDERTONE, BUT THE MUSTARD COLOR
ENRICHES THE OTHERWISE NEUTRAL PALETTE OF PALE YELLOW.

ONCE BROWN, THESE
REEXECUTED FORMS
TAKE ON A MODERN
SENSIBILITY.

Given my penchant for chairs, it is no surprise that I have performed superficial surgeries throughout my own home. In my conservatory, I even painted Gustavian chairs because the white needed to be slightly dulled. In the dining room, the surgery was more invasive. Ten chairs were the final compromise in lieu of the desired twelve because it is almost impossible to find antique or vintage chairs in these multiples. I settled upon ten Louis XVI–style chairs that I found at an antiques shop. Their form was diminutive, but not as petite as their antique forebears; therefore, they would be comfortable for modern use. They were brown, covered in a puce and green corduroy, yet their forms were perfect in my mind. I had them painted semigloss black and reupholstered in white kid leather, and their front sides were adorned with burnished nail heads. On the back, which is perhaps the more important side, as this is how dining room chairs are predominantly viewed, I used a striped fabric with the same background color as the white of the leather on the front of the chairs. Finally, I added vintage handles to the back to enhance interest and function when moving the chairs.

Because refinishing is often possible, I strongly encourage you to keep an open mind as you shop. I have discovered some of my dearest possessions in the most unlikely venues. You need not be a designer to see potential. Look for beautiful objects that could be reinvigorated if painted rather than dismissing them in their perhaps "pre-Pygmalion" state. The form is what you have to appreciate when you come upon it. (Of course, I do not recommend painting precious antiques or, for that matter, furniture pieces that have such sentimental value that altering them would compromise that moment in time.)

Another distinctive form that caught my eye was a mirror I found for a client's foyer. The large oval frame was so appealing because two candle arms were part of the original carved frame. It would be perfect in the foyer, where it would reflect the two front French doors. There was just one problem: my client had made it clear that the only thing she did not care for was anything vibrantly gilt. But because the form was so perfect and ideal for the space, I suggested that we could dull the finish. She agreed, so we had the frame painted dark bronze by a decorative painter, and it now graces the foyer.

My house is filled with furniture pieces that I knew I could redefine with paint. These objects give me the greatest thrill. Why? Because I feel like I have "rescued" or "discovered" something that was not understood or recognized by others, who simply passed it by. I had a precious Asian armoire in my dining room, but I always thought its scale did not fit the room. I felt that this piece, though beautiful as an object standing alone, never suited the space. There was no urgency to replace it, because it was relatively expensive, and I did not want to be indiscriminate or wasteful. I opted therefore to live with it for some time.

While on a shopping trip in Pennsylvania, I spotted what I thought would be its perfect replacement. The piece was a nineteenth-century Belgian pine

FEW BUT
ALL HIGHLY
RELEVANT
PIECES WERE
PLACED IN THIS
ENTRY FOYER.

armoire. As I set upon it, I thought, "I hope this thing isn't obscenely expensive." Thankfully it was not. The proportions were extreme, so my lust for it was measured as I thought to myself, "It will never make the stairs in my house." I also wondered if its transportation cost would defeat the bargain. As luck would have it, it was manageable by a matter of inches. The piece was a great bargain, and because it was not so precious in its original form, paint would not compromise its value.

To this day, it remains one of my favorite pieces in the house. I had the armoire painted semigloss black on the outside. The interior allowed me to take a bit of a "walk on the wild side." I had been toying with the idea of painting the dining room orange, but none of my colleagues thought this was a good idea as I would surely be sorry if I did. So the compromise would be an orange interior for the armoire. I have to say I'm glad I landed there. When I've had enough orange, I can close the door. I took a sponge-tipped brush and mixed brown and pale yellow together to create a bronze gilt to detail it myself, because overall the armoire was primitive and therefore might have been corrupted if placed in the care of an exacting decorative painter. In one hand, I had the sponge brush, and in the other a paper towel to dull the paint the very moment that it was applied to the faint mold detail that I was articulating.

What better way to define your home than by using your own hands? I have found that this approach to decorating is perhaps among the most immediately gratifying. I promise I'm not anyone's weekend warrior project guy, but every now and then it is frankly therapeutic for me to play in paint. Try it.

ABOVE: ALSO ON THE ARMOIRE WITH THE ORANGE INTERIOR, FOUND CASEMENT WINDOW HARDWARE SERVES AS AN INNOVATIVE DOORSTOP.

OPPOSITE: THANKFULLY THE ORANGE DOOR CLOSES. I WAS NOT CERTAIN I WOULD ALWAYS EMBRACE THIS BOLD COLOR MOVE.

TEXTILES

Textiles should be approached with just as much care and consideration as paints. They too act as connective tissue throughout the home. I personally gravitate toward fabrics that have a soft hand, muted colors, and understated patterns. These complement the soothing hues that I prefer. I like matte textiles such as linen, cotton, and suede, with the occasional velvet and chenille, because the hand of these fabrics is inherently welcoming. Just as form plays a critical role with furniture you might be hoping to redefine with paint, it is just as important with furniture you might want to redefine with upholstery. I have found that discreet patterns and textiles used on the reverse can do much to create a calm atmosphere within a room as compared with more active motifs and vibrant shades. Given the amount of chaos in the world, I like coming home to a calm retreat achieved through soothing paints and textiles.

TRAINING YOUR EYE: CARPETS AND AREA RUGS

Here are a few details worth considering when identifying carpets and area rugs.

1. Consider the following when selecting a rug size:
   - Is there a fireplace hearth?
   - Is there a pattern on the floor (hardwood border and so forth)?
   - Are there any floor vents or returns that cannot be blocked?
   - Think about the thickness of the material: will you have issues with doors swinging over the top or furniture placement on the rug?

2. Play with layering your area rugs.
   - Sometimes I prefer placing antique rugs on their well-worn reverse. They are more approachable given the sense of wear. Likewise they are more faded and prone to blend rather than compete with a subdued color palette.
   - Layering this type of rug with a natural-fiber underlayment, such as sisal, serves a similar purpose to framing a beautiful piece of artwork.

3. The pattern and color choices are endless, but consider the following:
   - A woven texture or an antique rug can add subtle pattern to a room without being overwhelming.
   - A subtle discreet nod to the wall color is often preferred.

A RECLAIMED WROUGHT-IRON PENDANT AT THE CENTER OF THE FAMILY ROOM IS A PERFECT FOIL TO THE BILLARD CLOTH DRAPERY.

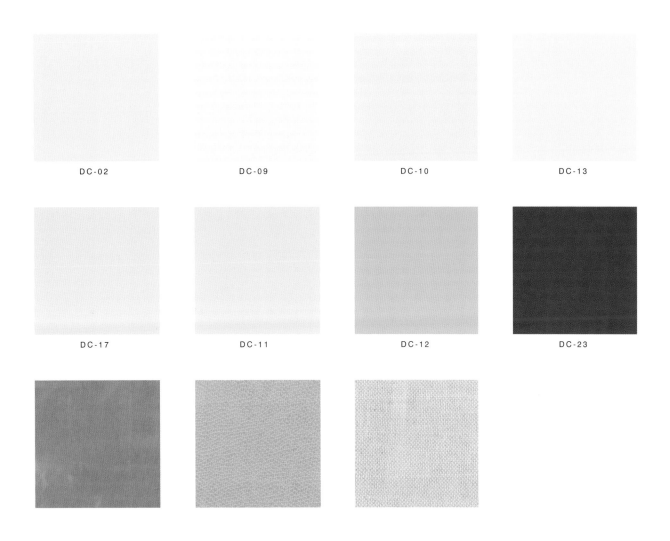

DC-02 DC-09 DC-10 DC-13

DC-17 DC-11 DC-12 DC-23

THE SUBTLE MOVEMENT IN THIS WALLPAPERED ALCOVE WAS INSPIRED
BY THE SURROUNDING FOLIAGE. THE BACKGROUND OF THIS PAPER
WAS PURPOSELY CHOSEN TO RELATE TO THE SOOTHING PALE ECRU
WALL COLOR IN THE NEIGHBORING GUEST BEDROOM.

DC-03 DC-06 DC-33 DC-34

DC-35 DC-07 DC-36 DC-48

A HOME'S COLOR PALETTE SHOULD HAVE A SENSE OF COHESION
THROUGHOUT. THIS STUDY HAS A SIMILAR PALETTE TO THAT OF
THE SECOND-FLOOR LANDING ON PAGE 136. BUT IN THIS ROOM,
THE COLORS ARE FAR MORE SATURATED. THE CABINET BACKS ARE
UPHOLSTERED IN A PALE-YELLOW AND ACID-GREEN TOILE. PATTERN
CAN BE SUBTLY INTRODUCED INTO A SPACE WITHOUT READING AS
OVERWHELMING.

COLLECT

7

SEEK THE ARTISANAL IN FURNITURE

Once the envelope of your home is established, now comes the fun of collecting your furnishings. This layering of the home is an ever-evolving process, and it offers the truest overall expression of your personality. While the making of the house must be logic driven, it should also be heart-felt. Equally important as textile selection is the furniture it will reside upon. Furniture most strongly sets the tone for how your home will be experienced.

THE PAINTED MILL TREATMENT LIBERATES THIS
TUDOR HOUSE AND PROVIDES A WELCOMING
BACKGROUND IN THE FOYER.

Remember, there is no such thing as perfection. A preoccupation with all things unblemished is certain to cause frustration and to produce a house too precious to enjoy. Embrace signs of wear and of the human hand on your furniture. Integrate artisanal gestures. Such evidence of age and craftsmanship is what brings character and authenticity to a home. When guests enter your home and encounter timeworn patinas, they intuitively relax. The weathered finishes subliminally suggest a house is lived in rather than preserved as an untouchable museum.

In the various houses you visit, notice how some will welcome you while others will intimidate. The home decor market nods to this way of thinking in the noticeable proliferation of new things made to look old. Freshly manufactured furniture and objects can be delivered to your home preworn just as denim is prewashed. Machine-made dings and roughed-up paint suggestive of use—the precise machine-made process of artificially making things look old—is a rather ridiculous response. Integrating found, timeworn pieces into a home can quietly effect a sense of the bygone. These gestures are not necessarily costly and can turn a mundane room that is otherwise a drywall box into an intimate gathering place.

As you begin collecting your home, shop thoughtfully. If something speaks to you, recognize that so long as it fits the general spirit and scale of your home, it can migrate to a new location as the furniture plan develops.

THE CALM
OF THE HARP-
BACKED CHAIR
COUNTER-
BALANCES THE
MOVEMENT OF
THE CANVAS.

SCALE

When considering your furnishings, think about them in the context of the whole house, in the space where you'll be placing them, and in relation to other nearby objects. The scale of furnishings is essential, whether in a spare environment, where each piece needs to be highly relevant, or in a more generously populated environment, where objects are more prone to interact with one another.

Similar logic will apply to the size and scale of the house and its rooms. Larger rooms may be better served with more furniture pieces placed in more intimate arrangements within that room. So try to resist the instinct to place a large sofa in a family room, where two smaller sofas facing each other may better encourage interaction. In a small bedroom, your first instinct might be to buy a small bed. By contrast, I often like to place a four-poster bed with narrow testers. The dimensions of the bed almost fill the space, yet visually the form is unobtrusive. We've also added built-in bookcases with a slide-out tray that doubles as a night table. Using every inch of your space in a small room and multifunctional furniture will help you create an aesthetically pleasing, comfortable space.

RHYTHM

If and where possible, try to create a sense of rhythm throughout your home. Just because a family room is an active public space does not preclude an occasional antique or primitive piece, particularly if it fits the overall spirit of the house. Likewise, relate the interior to the exterior of the house. If the paint on your home's exterior is visible from the inside, you can use muted window treatments that echo the exterior paint color. Or if your windows look out on wooded property, a muted floral drapery may connect the inside with the outside. The experience of the home should be seamless. In a large family room, heavier window treatments rather than lighter ones can render the environment more intimate and comfortable.

One of the more memorable rooms I have encountered, where the envelope was intact, was a graceful 1920s oval dining room. Even without any embellishment, the space was stunningly appealing; the room seemed to naturally envelop

THE COFFEE TABLE FROM THE CLIENT'S FORMER RESIDENCE WAS TOO SMALL TO SUIT THE NEW SPACE. WHEN IT WAS ENLARGED, THE ORIGINAL CLEFT METAL EDGE OF THE BASE WAS EXTENDED THROUGHOUT THE ADDITION.

you. All it really needed was a dining table that would follow its contour. The desired piece was instantly clear in my vision, and likewise in my memory, as I had seen it somewhere. Thankfully we found it. Because there was such a precise relationship between the table and the shape of the room, to avoid over-design, a table with a primitive quality was preferable. The chairs opposite the table could stand to be a bit haute gilt, but the chair forms would need to differ slightly to support the flow and dialogue of the room. Mixing the chairs up a bit and leaving the envelope as it was created a lazy elegance of natural rhythm to the room.

VISUAL CONTRAST

When it comes to arranging furniture, art, and accent pieces, sometimes the careful pairing of opposites can produce an appealing visual creative tension that results in a sense of harmony and balance. Objects can provide a sense of conversation among them. The goal is to gather pieces that deliberately yet discreetly relate to one another. The differences between them can enhance the sense of dialogue that will be shared. I have a visual tendency toward contrasts. I like to pair the modern with the antique, the refined opposite the primitive, amusing art near serious sculpture. This logic may be confounding, as it is far easier to place together things that "match." When you're collecting furnishings for your home, take chances, and mix things up. You will be delighted with the unexpected outcome once the at-large spirit of the home is established.

NOTICE THE CONVERSATION BETWEEN
THE CHAIRS IN THIS OVAL DINING ROOM.

ABOVE: THE CANDLE BRACKETS OF THE
DELICATE FORGED METAL CANDLESTICK
CAN BE MOVED UP AND DOWN.

OPPOSITE: THE JUXTAPOSITION
OF MODERN AND ANTIQUE CREATES
VISUAL TENSION AND ILLUSTRATES
DISCIPLINED ECLECTICISM.

Try to experience your house like a visitor, whose first impression is formed in the foyer. Foyers can be very challenging. A large foyer is still a hallway, and a hallway should routinely be treated as such. By this I mean that these spaces serve a purpose. They are generally not intended as resting places but rather greeting or receiving spaces, so passage and traffic are critical obvious considerations. A table to suit the size of the space, art that can be appreciated in the space, a vessel for fresh flowers, a rug to sustain traffic, a chair or bench in case it's needed, candles if desired. These are the basics for all different entry spaces.

The following foyers give you some examples. The first illustrates the idea of visual tension. In the hallway entry of a beautiful apartment, I placed an ornately hand-carved eighteenth-century Tuscan table discovered on one of many shopping trips. I layered it with a plaster female torso that the homeowner had acquired long ago and a glass vessel to welcome the homeowner and visitors with seasonal flowers. A contrast is provided by the modern white zigzag chair, an element no one would expect, yet the story of the home begins here.

In one large foyer, a distinctive nineteenth-century piano case, relieved of its instrument, had perfect proportions to suit the space as a side table. Its gravity was counterbalanced by an intricate seventeenth-century Flemish tapestry. Both of these objects echoed the Italianate character of the house.

NOTE THE UNEXPECTED PAIRING OF AN ANTIQUE CHAISE AND A DISTINCTIVE SADDLE STONE PLACED ON A SIMPLE WHITE PEDESTAL. OPPOSITES ATTRACT.

In a Tudor entry, a typical wainscot treatment executed in white serves to enhance the presence of so many beautiful objects. A rare antique English grandfather clock with a white face, mahogany case, and eight-day bell strike, circa 1820, and a Swedish mahogany table with an oval pedestal base, circa 1830, look natural together. The stool in front is a graceful gesture that can support overflow seating in any of the public rooms. The spare environment obliges the few important pieces; a clear cylindrical vase heaped with hydrangea feels welcoming.

Next, consider an inner foyer, a formal setting with a Georgian period table, circa 1780, that is remarkably modern in the company of a highly ornate mirror and a chinoiserie-style armchair. The early reproduction mirror had a gilt finish, but it was not precious, so we could paint it black without compromise. The form took on a graphic, abstract quality against the white wall. The nineteenth-century Chinese chair is also rather modern in this placement. These pieces have an extraordinary dialogue.

While not a foyer, the upper landing in a Tudor also illustrates visual contrast. The space is unified by milled wainscot that travels up the primary stairs and onto the second-floor landing. The architecture of this home is truly magnificent and ever so demure at once. Its furnishings needed to be true to the homeowner and respectful of the architecture.

On a shopping trip in London, my client and I discovered so many precious things, among them several period mantels and a set of four nineteenth-century iron dragon wall sconces. We used them progressing up the stairs and at the top of the landing, where two of them flank a rare American Grecian-style mahogany chaise, circa 1820. An unusual saddle stone elevated on a pedestal sits on one side of the chaise. Polar opposites, they coexist nicely together. The chaise confidently reclines with a sheepish grin, fully aware of its elegance. The saddle stone on a painted white base purposefully balances the pretense of the chaise in this composition.

THE GEORGIAN TABLE HAS AN
ANIMATED QUALITY ABOUT IT. I
CAN IMAGINE ITS LEGS MOVING.

DEFINING PIECES

It is not uncommon for me to find a single piece that will define the entire character of the design of a house. In one instance, a client's kitchen was still on the drawing board. In general, kitchens should share some sense of the at-large design vocabulary of the home. I thought that an antique French baker's table incorporated into the kitchen island might be just such a defining piece, because it related to the rest of the home. I added a honed stone top to the primitive table, which was just what it needed. The stone refined and elevated that piece and its utility. Plus the baker's table served as a focal point in the kitchen and greatly relieved the static regiment of milled cabinetry around the room's perimeter. Knowing that various handsome antiques would adorn the rest of the house, I felt the kitchen needed one at its epicenter.

Sometimes you can integrate a small piece of furniture into a larger one and give it new life. My firm had one client whose father was a contemporary of George Nakashima, the renowned furniture maker. Under his training, the father had made a small coffee table, which had been in storage for years. Naturally, this was a keepsake. The scale of the table, however, was too small for the intended room. In fact, when we went to visit the storage facility, where it had been sequestered most of the homeowner's adult life, the client joked about how large the table had seemed from his childhood memory. Now, it was dwarfed by his six-foot, five-inch frame. To redefine the original table to suit the space, we enlarged it by commissioning a bigger white metal box around it on three sides and leaving the top and the legs of the original smaller table exposed on one side. In effect, this treatment provided the necessary mass for the space while both honoring and preserving the original table.

ABOVE: AS IT WAS CREATED UNDER THE TRAINING OF GEORGE NAKASHIMA, THE SMALLER TABLE IS A VERY IMPORTANT KEEPSAKE THAT NEEDED TO BE PROMINENTLY PLACED. THE LIVING ROOM CALLED FOR A LARGER TABLE, AND SO THESE NEEDS WERE MARRIED.

OPPOSITE: THE FRENCH BAKER'S TABLE WAS ENGAGED AS PART OF THIS KITCHEN ISLAND TO ADD BOTH INTEREST AND UTILITY.

ABOVE: THE INFRASTRUCTURE OF THE CHAIR IMMEDIATELY INTRIGUED ME.

OPPOSITE: THE SCREEN WAS PERFECTLY INDULGENT IN THIS MASTER BEDROOM.

BEDROOMS

When collecting furniture for your bedroom, keep the following guidelines in mind. Despite the common temptation toward overstatement in a large bedroom, in my view, bedrooms in many styles benefit from a calm and logical design approach. The bed will routinely dominate the space, no matter its size. The bed should be either over- or underwhelming, either receding into the architecture by its low profile or flagrantly celebrated with posts, testers, and all. There may be an armoire if a television is present. If you can have either a fireplace or an armoire, a fireplace trumps a TV in my mind. If you have to have a television, avoid suspending it above the fireplace unless you can have it cleverly integrated into a hidden cavity within the architecture.

Bedside tables are far more visually interesting when they do not match; the occupant who has more "stuff" should win the larger one. If you don't have a large table beside the bed, find a home elsewhere in the room and pull two companion reading chairs up to it. These too should have individual personalities.

If you have space for art, you must really love what you choose, as it will bid you goodnight and greet you in the morning. When appropriate to the architecture, folding screens can lend a great sense of volume, interest, and intimacy to a larger bedroom. They have a very distinct presence and voice. Sometimes they are simple and upholstered, other times they are precious works of art . . . dark, painterly, romantic.

I am not one to disparage an occasional impulse purchase. If a piece speaks to you provocatively, you might buy it simply because you have to have it. I purchased a chair in my bedroom purely because its exposed infrastructure intrigued me. The chair is a remnant of a three-part tête-à-tête. While this defies logic, I bought this chair because I liked the way it looked from the back. I had the infrastructure painted black—very carefully—because I was determined to preserve the original burlap on the back of the chair. And I had the front upholstered in white linen. For me, this chair is art, sculpture, architecture, and, coincidentally, furniture.

TABLES

Tables in certain parts of the home, such as the living room and dining room, command center stage, so these need to be chosen or designed with careful consideration for space and use. Regrettably, dining rooms are often treated as trophy rooms, when they could be gathering places that encourage a spirit of conviviality with fantastic food and conversation. In this regard, the materials of the table become an essential factor. My own dining room has served as a veritable laboratory over the years. I have had glass tables, which are a nightmare to keep clean, prone to scratches, and too revealing for the comfort of guests. I have had precious antique tables that were beautiful, but I subconsciously winced every time a drinking glass was placed upon them.

Finally, and accidentally, I came upon a concrete table that was architecturally appealing and indestructible. At first glance, it was a bargain, too, until its shipping bill showed up. It took a makeshift crane to deliver it from a long wait in my foyer up the stairs to the dining room. This one is a keeper due to its weight alone. It was a simple concrete slab mounted on top of three innocuous cubes. Once I lived with it for a while, my propensity to want to redefine things in my care kicked in. Now that I had a more welcoming and durable table, I discovered a need to accommodate a larger group. Thus the artful intervention of a leaf at the end attached to a new angular base—this was now a dining table that was sculpture.

The need for greater vision and design is why I always engage artists or artisans wherever possible in the design process. I have turned to my colleague Margaret Boozer for many projects over the years. Within moments of being in her studio, in her company and surrounded by so many organic materials and mediums, I experience a catharsis. Margaret is an exceptional artist with a creative mind and the discipline of an engineer.

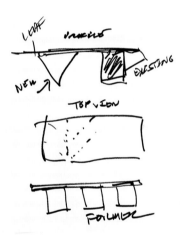

ABOVE: MY MIND AT WORK . . . HOW TO MAKE MY DINING ROOM TABLE LONGER?

OPPOSITE: THE PROTOTYPE OF MY DINING ROOM TABLE "ADDITION" AND THE FINAL RESULT.

In this case, I called upon Margaret to fashion an intervening material to lengthen my dining room table and improve the overall design of the piece. I made an adolescent hand drawing of how I hoped it would be executed. Margaret laughed at me and the design and asked me quite seriously if I had any clue as to how the properties of the materials proposed actually work. After she gave me a science lesson, we tackled the project in our (her) usual spirit. I wanted the table to appear to be gravity-defiant, but my original design to that end did not work. Thankfully, all my comrades embrace my insanity and the challenge.

For want of a more technical description, the extension is a metal sheet, which has a V-shaped blackened steel ribbon with its point resting on the floor for support. The extension is detachable if ever I should want to seat fewer guests. Suffice it to say, this table will remain in its place with the extension, at least during my stewardship of my present home.

Figuring out how to make a table suit a semicircular promenade next to a client's kitchen was another memorable challenge. That was the most logical space for the table, and it would afford a serene view of the pool. The space already served as an aesthetically pleasing passage, but the owners would enjoy it far more if a table could be used for seated gatherings.

A GRACIOUS PASSAGE BECAME FAR MORE ENJOYABLE AS A SEATING VENUE. THE TABLE DESIGN HAD TO BE EXACTING.

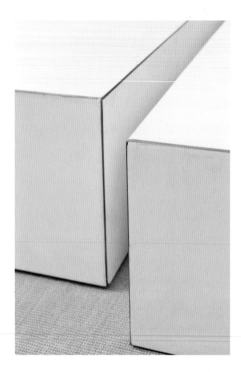

LESS IS MORE. THESE "SIMPLE" CUBES THAT SERVE AS MY LIVING ROOM COFFEE TABLES ARE ACTUALLY HIGHLY COMPLEX IN THEIR DESIGN.

As the client and I were shopping, we visited an importer I routinely deal with who works in Brazilian hardwoods. Though it is predominantly a retail establishment, the hard-hewn quality of its offerings has always appealed to me. With the promenade in mind, somehow we convinced the importer to construct a table that consisted of three sections so that it could fit on a barge and then on a delivery truck, and so that the assembled result would follow the contour of the room.

As you're shopping for tables, keep an eye out for coffee tables in particular. I have discovered that they can be some of the hardest pieces to select, because they can easily compromise a room. Coffee tables are often too small, too big, too short, too tall, or altogether do not suit a room's vocabulary. Less often, they are just right, unless and until you move them to a new space. It is frankly sometimes easier to adapt something you already have than to search for its replacement.

In my own living room, the coffee tables are a pair of low-profile asymmetric cubes. Nothing complicated other than the fact that they are made of paper-thin gypsum cement mounted to a metal infrastructure because that one-eighth inch of exposed metal edge faintly suggests its complex innards. Oh, and yes, I wanted them to be on wheels in case I was compelled to move them around. As you can see, furniture can also be art.

THE DISTINCTIVE
CHINOISERIE
CHEST, FOUND IN
LONDON, IS ALSO
FUNCTIONAL IN
THIS DINING ROOM.

suggestions for kitchens

When planning your kitchen, there are so many options to consider.

Think about your tolerance levels
for the following:

- Do you like everything to be put away—clean counters—or would you prefer open shelves for displaying your dishes and so forth?

- Would multiple workstations help direct the flow of the space?

- Would you like a place for kids to sit and watch food prep?

- Do you want to be near guests or secluded when cooking?

- Would you prefer to be able to close off the kitchen after food prep and while eating dinner?

- Do you have any need for televisions or computers integrated into the kitchen?

- Consider counter height when planning cabinet installation. It may be helpful to raise or lower counter heights to fit individuals, but keep resale in mind when planning.

Think about the following when
choosing your countertop and
backsplash material:

- View the full slab when selecting the stone for your countertop or backsplash—many stones have veining that may not appear on a small sample.

- Even synthetic materials may vary in color from one piece to the next, so it is important to see each piece before installation.

- Do you find watermarks acceptable or a nuisance? Perhaps this should guide your countertop material selection. Ask to take a sample home and spill things on it to see if stains result.

- Consider the size of the grout lines on tile backsplashes when determining how easily the tile will clean.

For sinks and appliances:

- Consider kitchen sink utility and if you need more than one type.

- What sink depth do you prefer for washing large pots, pans, and the like?

- What about adding a prep sink or a pot filler at the stove?

- Consider operating sink(s) with a foot pedal.

- Is there a need for water filtration connected to your sink and/or ice maker?

- How will the sink be cleaned? Perhaps a sprayer may be useful.

- Would a built-in soap dispenser at the sink be convenient?

- Consider how you use appliances and if you would like to add additional ones.

- Review all appliance specifications to determine if there are any special power or plumbing requirements.

- What about adding a built-in coffee station or hot-water dispenser for tea to start your day off?

- When planning the location, think about access to water and garbage.

- How about a wine refrigerator or a refrigerator drawer for kids' snacks?

- How often do you entertain? Are multiple dishwashers or ovens needed to accommodate the volume?

- Which cooking method do you prefer: gas versus electric (or a combination); convection oven; microwave oven; built-in rotisserie?

Consider your storage needs and think about how you use your kitchen:

- How do you buy and store food? Do you freeze a lot or use only fresh ingredients? Consider needs for extra freezer or refrigeration space.

- If you are an avid home cook, you may want to consider the orientation of implements that you need more immediate access to and place them accordingly.

- Where will interior waste bins best traffic to exterior waste bins?

- A pantry may be needed for large quantities of food. Perhaps a secondary pantry in another location is also an option.

8

CURATE

SELECT MEANINGFUL ART

When you're collecting art and accents for your home, be innovative and open to exploring nontraditional opportunities. Art, like beauty, is in the eye of the beholder. The places that I find art and furnishings are often as unlikely as the pieces I find there. I have found a nineteenth-century piano in Wisconsin, a Burmese chain in South Carolina, a pair of Foo Dogs in Denmark, and a factory machinist's table in the United Kingdom. As I mentioned earlier, I enjoy scouring architectural reclamation yards, flea markets, and other off-the-beaten-path venues. I encourage you to do the same. Also, allow yourself an occasional guilty pleasure. Maybe the indulgent painting will have such presence in the anticipated room that it will suggest that fewer furniture pieces need to reside in its company. If so, your purchase is justified, if not encouraged.

A PERFECT DIALOGUE BETWEEN
UNLIKE COMPANIONS.

AN ORMOLU CLOCK RESTS ON AN
HEIRLOOM CHEST OF DRAWERS
AND IS THE COUNTERBALANCE
TO THE MASCULINITY THAT
PERMEATES THIS APARTMENT.

The reason I tend toward spare environments is that they allow each object to take on its own importance. While on one hand, the curation of these spaces must be exacting, this simplicity also gives license for placement of objects that would otherwise be egregiously over the top. The secret is that you don't need a lot of things; you need a few really good things. I am truly not a fan of the banal, and often just when a room's vocabulary seems to be predictable, I will unapologetically throw a curveball. In my own home, for instance, the art seems benign enough if it is simply viewed as part of the atmosphere. If studied, however, my abstracts can be quite provocative. The beauty of the abstract is that it is most often left to the viewer to discern—inviting much lively discussion. I have a running joke that I am color blind, because art dealers often presume to show me works that are "gestural" in neutrals like black, brown, and beige. I find these colors generally pleasing, but art must stand alone, not simply visually complement an environment. It must evoke thought, laughter, and conversation.

This spirit sometimes comes as a shock to my clients. I will never forget the reaction of one of my clients when I presented a frankly pretentious nineteenth-century gilt ormolu clock replete with a cupid supporting its face. When I saw this clock while shopping, I knew I was going to get just the reaction that I did. The apartment is quite masculine in its vocabulary, and this clock was wholly inconsistent with its style, and, in a way, it was poking fun at it. My client got that, and he embraced the humor in the contrast. Look for the uncommon things, those that make you laugh, or better yet, quietly amuse you as you watch others take them in. These objects cannot be found in a catalog; they must be original or privately entertaining.

CONCRETE
LIONS PROUDLY
PROTECT
THE MODERN
SCULPTURE
BENEATH—A
COMPOSITION
OF A BENCH AND
CUBES CRAFTED
OF ANCIENT
TEAK THAT
WAS EBONIZED
TO SUIT ITS
MODERN
CONTEXT.

Recently I became intrigued with some industrial pierced metal skids that had been used to capture residue, the spoils of the artisanal plaster-making process, because they seemed almost like rings defining the life span of a tree. I was intrigued by the buildup, the aftermath of so many unknown plaster pieces that speak from these skids. The by-product of the making of art would now be suspended on a wall as art in its own right.

I share this so that you, too, will look at things from all different angles, especially objects that are meaningful to you and things that you wouldn't typically think of as art. Then the key is to figure out creative ways to display them. For instance, one of my clients inherited his father's antique bookbinding tools, which included a pair of long, rectangular wooden blocks connected by threaded metal dowels. We hung these sideways in an entry hall, and at first glance, it's not apparent what they are. Because they look intriguing, they often ignite conversation.

WHAT WERE ONCE ARTISAN SKIDS
WITH AGGREGATE RESIDUE FROM THE
PLASTER-MAKING PROCESS BECAME
ART THEMSELVES AS A QUADTYCH.

ABOVE: THE GRAVITY OF THE SCONCES SUGGESTED A LOW PLACEMENT JUST ABOVE THE CHAIR RAIL AND HELPED GIVE A HUMAN SCALE TO THE ROOM.

OPPOSITE: ONE SOLUTION FOR A PASSAGE THAT FEELS NARROW IS TO PLACE ART THAT VISUALLY INTEGRATES WITH THE ARCHITECTURE.

PROPORTION

The placement of various decorative objects can affect the way a room feels. I was searching for a way to give human scale to a large dining room with high ceilings when I found a nineteenth-century French trumeau mirror, probably reclaimed from a Parisian flat. It honors the space without being overwhelming. The wall sconces, which are large and ornate, relate to the bas-relief design in the mirror, echoing a similar design upside down. I hung the sconces lower than normal to create the illusion of lowering the high ceiling.

For a city apartment, I found an 1870 plaster relief depicting the Greek goddess of the hunt, Artemis. Because it was diminutive, my colleagues and I originally planned to place it above the bedroom headboard. However, the art placement above the bed needed to be impactful while not competing for center stage with the beautiful upholstered headboard.

Even the framers we use are artists. I realized the relief had the gravity to hold a far more important place in the apartment: the elegant entry hallway. Everything in the space was selected to bow to the architecture. Once the small relief was amplified in several feet of white matting and attached to a solid understructure, it was perfectly fitting. The relief is far more engaging in this presentation, and although the finished artwork is large in this execution, it recedes into the architecture.

THIS COMPOSITION
BALANCES ORNAMENT
AND SIMPLICITY.

MAKE A STATEMENT

Certain areas of your home that may seem awkward, such as powder rooms, actually provide opportunities to indulge your guests and take some chances. Because powder rooms are routinely small, this is where you may opt for more precious wallpapers or hand-painted walls or other rarer wall treatments.

In my own powder room, I have covered the walls in framed cartoons that each defame the design process. I cannot tell you how many of my guests yank me aside after reading those cartoons. It almost inspires a sense of a secret society, and it is fascinating to me to discover who gravitates toward which comic.

Powder rooms are also the unapologetic bastion of garish mirrors, as they should be. And because garish does not mean precious, this is one instance where so many different frames can work. Paint can really redefine flea market finds in this context. You can also experiment widely with vanities here. I often create vanities out of an antique console or small chest suspended on legs, adapting the top with stone to install a sink. An ornate console can be tempered by a mirror that is not too fussy, depending upon your tastes.

If you are bashful about too much opulence, then consider a closet as your laboratory for recklessness. Here wallpaper can be safely sequestered. Nonetheless, you'll want to thoughtfully choose patterns and colors that are classic. My own foyer guest closet is papered in a black and gilt chinoiserie pattern.

MY OWN POWDER ROOM IS VERY TELLING IF YOU CAREFULLY READ THE FRAMED COMICS THAT COVER ITS WALLS. MOST OF THEM POKE FUN AT THE DESIGN PROCESS, SUCH AS "THE NEED FOR PERENNIALS TO MATCH EXACTLY THE PAINT COLOR ON THE SHUTTERS OF THE HOUSE."

TRAINING YOUR EYE: COLLECTING

When beginning a collection, gather objects that have continuity in their form; for example, a collection of buttons or pottery. Keeping your collection focused will create visual harmony. When items are too disparate they can register as visual clutter rather than a curated collection. Flow blue, ironstone, and intaglios are among the objects I collect. Once you decide what your collection will be, vary the sizes and styles. For example, my collection of flow blue consists of plates, platters, bowls, and pitchers.

When displaying your collections, group them together to make a statement. A piece or two here and there may get lost among the other items in your home. Frame your smaller collected items with discipline, either together in one large frame or in many different frames of the same size, style, and color. Hang your framed collections in unexpected locations such as an empty hall or under an open stair. The absence of other items around your collection will give importance to its singular placement.

ABOVE: HERE YOU CAN SEE A RANGE OF IMAGERY AND SIZES AMONG MY INTAGLIO COLLECTION, GROUPED TOGETHER FOR DISPLAY WITHIN AN ANTIQUE FELT LINEN JEWELRY DISPLAY CASE I SALVAGED FROM A LOCAL CONSIGNMENT SHOP.

OPPOSITE: BOLDLY PATTERNED WALLPAPER IS A PLEASANT SURPRISE FOR GUESTS.

The spaces where you actively live in your house should be the most thoughtful in their design. Their decoration should transcend the physical appointments of the space. Is there a favorite scent that refreshes you? Something as simple as a candle may be desirable.

Be sure to try out new ideas. Until relatively recently, I was the enforcer of the white candle. I still think this is always the best and most appropriate solution for candles. But I must admit that black candles look great atop a pair of nineteenth-century bronze candelabras.

In short, use your home as a place for self-expression. View it as a canvas and each decision as one more brushstroke toward that final composition. It may forever be a work in progress. Perhaps that's just how it should be. I will always advocate things done well slowly over things done poorly instantly. This is the essence of collecting the home.

THE MODERN ART IS A
PLEASING FOIL TO THE
TUFTED FORM OF THE
CHESTERFIELD SOFA.

suggestions for lighting

Among the many details to examine when you approach lighting are the following:

- Consider where to locate junction boxes for pendants, chandeliers, and sconces.

- Will heavy-duty junction boxes or blocking (wood supports) be required for overhead fixtures to accommodate weight?

- Often antique sconces have smaller back plates—it is important to verify the dimensions when purchasing the sconces so the necessary preparations can be made.

- If sconces with back plates smaller than standard sizes are going to be used, coordination with a general contractor/electrician is needed to identify the appropriate solution to meet code requirements.

- Consider adding electrical receptacles for floor lamps and/or other items that will "float" in a room.

- To determine the desired location for a floor receptacle, it is helpful to develop your furniture plan first. A floor receptacle would be better suited under a large piece of furniture that will hide it rather than in the middle of a pathway.

- Coordinate your preferred floor outlet locations with your general contractor/electrician, who can help you determine if this placement is possible based on the locations of existing floor joists. Once construction is under way, it is difficult and costly to move the receptacles, so planning ahead is critical.

- Consider the location of light switches as well as the thermostat and alarm controls. When possible, avoid placing them in the middle of a wall that could otherwise be used for art.

- Consider adding dimmable switches or a lighting control system. Soft light sets the ambience of a room. While it may be important to be able to turn the lights all the way up for cleaning, you would not want to host a dinner party under such conditions.

9

EVOLVE

EMBRACE LIFE'S CHANGES

As you and your family live, grow, and change, so too must your home. Here, we'll discuss how to integrate flexibility into your designs so you'll be able to evolve with the changes life will bring. New partnerships may be formed if you are single, families may grow, children will go off to explore their own lives, aging parents may move in with you. Through any or all of these, you'll want to maintain a forward-thinking approach to collecting your home.

IN THIS LIVING ROOM, GATHERING PLACES
FOR CHILDREN CLEVERLY SUIT THE LARGER
VOCABULARY OF THE ROOM.

FOUNDATIONS FOR NURSERIES

Even when you are considering a newborn's room, the space should have a foundation that can last. Though your impulse will naturally be to celebrate the arrival of your new family member, decorating the nursery should not be done impulsively, nor does the room necessarily need to reflect gender.

I have witnessed firsthand the excitement and desire to create the perfect nest, which can lead to too much input from grandmamas-to-be and all others imposing their own experience. I stand by my advice in *The New Traditional*: design by large committee is asking for trouble. Tell your entire opinionated posse that you have hired a decorator. (They don't need to know that it's you.) This no doubt will offend some people, but you will bask in your autonomy.

Rest assured that it is really all right to base a nursery on a calm, gender-neutral palette. Wallpapers can be muted—khakis, blues, or pale greens—and then you can adorn the room with age-appropriate trims or accents that can gradually be replaced once outgrown. Bookshelves can also be painted in a neutral or white. Newborns' rooms will become playful with the abundance of toys, mobiles, art, and gifts.

This approach will provide future flexibility. For instance, we once designed a nursery intended for a baby boy with pale blue, faintly discernable hatched wallpaper that would also be suitable if there was a future girl in the offing. The textile palette for the baby boy's room consisted of soft blue chenille, white percale crib bedding, white draperies with navy velvet trim, and pale gray and blue geometric trims and embellishments.

THE PALE-BLUE PALETTE OF THIS BOY'S ROOM WAS LIKEWISE SUITABLE FOR A GIRL'S ROOM ONCE NEW TRIMS AND FLORAL BED HANGINGS WERE ADDED.

A few years later, when his sister came along, he graduated into a bedroom with his older brother, and the accent and trim textiles in the former nursery were easily changed. We replaced the former trims and embellishments with floral accents. Bed hangings were added to make the room more fanciful, a mobile of white butterflies and beads was suspended from the ceiling, and horse prints were replaced by watercolors of angels. But the predominant neutral backgrounds—the base wallpaper and fabrics—survived because they were not gender or color defined. The textiles were youthful, yes, but they were chosen so that they could last well into childhood.

KIDS' ROOMS

Children's rooms can be quite an investment, so my colleagues and I do our best to neutralize them with classic color palettes. Even when our clients' children are very outspoken, we try to tone things down a bit. For instance, if a four-year-old says she wants everything to be hot pink, we persuade her that pale pink is more "grown-up" and that she may not tire of it as quickly as she might tire of the brighter shade. We want to create spaces our "little clients" will love, but we also want to make rooms that will last.

If we are upholstering the walls in precious fabric, we will steer away from childish motifs and encourage the selection of something more timeless, such as a toile with a pastoral design that can last into adolescence.

FOR THIS TODDLER'S BEDROOM,
PALE PINKS AND ACID GREENS WERE
COUPLED WITH MATURE FURNITURE
SO THAT THE ROOM WOULD LAST
THROUGH HER ADOLESCENCE.

We decorated one little girl's room with just such a lovely pink toile and accented the room with understated acid green, which was more sophisticated than anything she might have initially chosen. The scale of the patterns on all textiles was carefully selected and purposefully varied. And the values of the colors were more muted than what might routinely be placed in a child's room. A child's chair was paired with an adult chair, each executed in complementary colors and in different textiles—for the mother's chair, a pale pink linen seat and a large-scale green buffalo check on the back; for the daughter's chair, a similar pink linen on the seat and a small green gingham check on the back.

For a very mature six-year-old lad's room, we placed a queen-size sleigh bed sideways between bookcases that were populated with antique models of small cities, toy cars, maps, hourglasses, and all things that would inspire a young boy's mind. These will probably give way to trophies, textbooks, novels, and sports memorabilia. The bed placement was purposeful, with one long side nestled between the bookshelves. This way, the generously sized bed does not feel exposed like an island. The bed should last for years before the young boy outgrows it.

On the opposite side of this same room, we placed a desk at a window also flanked with bookshelves. Above the desk, we suspended a weighted billiard light fixture that adjusts up and down on a pulley system. The fixture will not be dwarfed as the boy grows to be tall like his father. The desk is set up as a true partner's desk, with a chair at either side. At this stage of the "little man's" life, the second chair can accommodate a parent, sibling, or friend for playing a

game or reading a book together. Later, the second chair may be used by a parent helping with homework or a classmate collaborating on a school project. Storage in this room is equally evolved—there is an antique leather campaign chest. All textiles selected for this room take their cue from men's suiting—pale blue and gray twills, blue and brown herringbone, and navy and turquoise cotton velvet. The wallpaper is a broad stripe responding to these colors—in this case a nod to men's shirting. These design decisions are logical. In both this six-year-old boy's room and the little girl's room described earlier, jarring wallpaper and vibrant patterns would have been outdated before the children had finished grade school.

SHARED BEDROOMS

Naturally, these same principles apply for siblings who share a room. For one set of brothers, we replaced their outgrown cribs with refined twin cane beds to see them through their teens. We used men's shirting–inspired fabrics with pale yellow stripes for draperies and bedcovers, and papered the walls in a wider pale yellow and gray stripe. We selected a tall, masculine chest of drawers to accommodate shared use, and an antique box for shared bedside storage. Antique coach lanterns provide lighting rather than something more childish.

MEN'S SHIRTING WAS THE INSPIRATION HERE.
THE ROOM TILTS TOWARD HABERDASHERY
FOR ITS "LITTLE GENTLEMEN."

ABOVE: AN EGALITARIAN SHARED
VANITY IS WELL PROPORTIONED
WHILE STILL PROVIDING ROOM FOR
MULTIPLE KIDS IN THE MORNINGS.

OPPOSITE: THOUGH THE ROOM IS
SHARED, EACH BOY CLAIMS A VERY
INDEPENDENT SPACE WITH BUNK BEDS
THAT ACT AS AN INDOOR TREEHOUSE.

Bunk beds are a great solution where there are two or more children who are close enough in age to share a room. A bunkroom capitalizes on every square inch of space. Rooms that may at first glance only sleep one or two can often sleep as many as four, depending upon the ceiling height and clever design. These spaces are particularly appealing to children; they often take on the feel of a tree house. Depending upon the execution, bunkrooms can give each child his or her own space, with bookcases built into the bed, each with its own separate wall sconce and control. In effect, these spaces can contain multiple independent retreats.

The goal is to give yourself some flexibility. As children grow, you don't want to have to redecorate from scratch for the different stages of their childhood. Rather, you want their rooms to evolve. And, who knows, as children move out into the world, you may have aging parents moving in. Such transitions will be easier if you integrate neutral colors, timeless patterns, and furnishings that can migrate from one space to another in your home because the scale throughout is consistent.

THIS SECOND-
FLOOR TERRACE
OFF MY KITCHEN
HAS BECOME
MY MORNING
RESPITE.

A PARTING WORD

As you have seen, collecting a home that pleases you and suits your needs will take time. We've discussed how thoughtful planning; careful selection of furnishings, finishes, and art; and allowing your home to evolve all play critical roles in creating a welcoming environment. In closing, I share one more story.

The second-floor terrace off my kitchen overlooks a park. Because I like to create intimate spaces that encourage conversation and I also wanted some privacy, I enclosed the side of my balcony to block the views into neighboring rear gardens with an iron trellis that is now covered in greenery. I collaborated with an artisan, who built triangular iron sides that come to a point, conjuring the sense of a tent. I planted foliage, talked to it, watered it, and waited impatiently for it to grow. Meanwhile, I had the dining-height table lowered so the space would be more engaging for gatherings. Eventually the greenery began to climb the trellis, growing thick enough to create the tranquil refuge I had envisioned.

Your home will not be collected overnight, but if treated with care and thoughtfully curated, it will be a treasure upon completion. Enjoy the journey.

APPENDIX A:
PAINTS

Images below may vary from true paint colors. To ensure color accuracy, apply actual paint samples to the surfaces and settings for which they are intended. For purchasing information regarding Darryl Carter Colors by Benjamin Moore, a list of which follows, visit www.darrylcarter.com.

DC-01
BANCROFT WHITE

DC-05
SOMERSET WHITE

DC-09
WILLARD WHITE

DC-02
HUNTINGTON
WHITE

DC-06
DOGUE GRAY

DC-10
GRANTHAM BLUE

DC-03
BONIFANT WHITE

DC-07
SHERIDAN GRAY

DC-11
ALBEMARLE BLUE

DC-04
CRESTRIDGE
WHITE

DC-08
ASHMEAD GRAY

DC-12
DALTON BLUE

DC-13
MAYFAIR WHITE

DC-17
TENNYSON WHITE

DC-21
PINECREST GRAY

DC-14
ELLSWORTH KHAKI

DC-18
FALLS WHITE

DC-22
PHELPS BLACK

DC-15
STRATTON KHAKI

DC-19
BROXBURN
GREIGE

DC-23
MARBURY BROWN

DC-16
WYTHE KHAKI

DC-20
ASHFORD GREIGE

DC-24
BAYARD BLUE

DC-25
LELAND WHITE

DC-26
BELMONT GRAY

DC-27
DELAFIELD GRAY

DC-28
ASHBY BLUE

DC-29
DUMBARTON
WHITE

DC-30
WHITEHAVEN BLUE

DC-31
GEORGETOWN
BLUE

DC-32
DRUMMOND BLUE

DC-33
CAMERON GREEN

DC-34
LINNEAN GREEN

DC-35
CLARENDON
GREEN

DC-36
DENTON GRAY

DC-37
HANOVER WHITE

DC-41
DECATUR WHITE

DC-45
TAMARACK GRAY

DC-38
FENWICK WHITE

DC-42
ESSEX YELLOW

DC-46
BULLOCK GRAY

DC-39
GRAFTON BROWN

DC-43
BLAGDON YELLOW

DC-47
CHASE GREEN

DC-40
BROOKDALE
BROWN

DC-44
DUNMORE
YELLOW

DC-48
VINTON BROWN

ARCHITECTS AND CONTRACTORS

Some of whom we've worked with and some of whom we look forward to working with (in alphabetical order)

- Barnes Vanze Architects, Inc.
- Peter Block Architects
- The Block Builders Group
- William Cromley Restoration
- Crone Associates Architects
- Cunningham | Quill Architects PLLC
- Duckworth Properties
- Franck & Lohsen Architects
- Gibson Builders, LLC
- Glass Construction

- Rene Gonzalez Architect
- Good Architecture
- GTM Architects
- Horizon Builders, Inc.
- Hutker Architects
- Ilex Construction and Woodworking
- isArk Studio
- Donald Lococo Architects
- Mauk & Zantzinger and Associates, Inc.
- Neumann Lewis Buchanan Architects

- PMI
- Sullivan Building & Design Group
- Michael F. Taylor, Inc.
- Russell Versaci Architecture
- Wade Weissmann Architecture, Inc.
- Richard Williams Architects
- Winchester Construction
- Wnuk Spurlock Architecture

SUPPORTERS, ARTISANS, AND TRADESPEOPLE

A special thanks to people and companies that make it possible and inspire me every day (in alphabetical order):

Ingrid Abramovitch • Jeffrey Akman • Jorge Arango • Margot Austin • Cris Barrett • Benjamin Moore • Sonya Bernhardt • Nisi Berryman • Lindsay Bierman • Barbara and Chip Bohl • Michael Boodro • Dennis Bowman • Jenny Bradley • Debra Brandt • The Brass Knob • Michael Bruno • Deborah Burns • Dara Caponigro • Giulio Capua • Jerry Carbonara • Catherine Casey • Jill Cohen • Rhonda Cole • Chuck Comeau • Janice Currie • Sherri Dalphonse • Sharon Dan • Ken Downing • Leslie Dunne Sadler • Coriline DuRant • Nicole Durfee • Amy Elbert • Carolyn Englefield • Milton Escobar • Sid Evans • Gretchen Everett • Brett Fahlgren • Pamela Fiori • John Flynn • Brittney Forrister • Martha Foulon-Tonat • Tony Freund • Tara Germinsky • Lester Gibretz • Gary Glant • Adam Glassman • Dan Golden • Laura Gottesman • Jamie Gould • Keith Granet • Charles Grazioli • Nick Greer • Linda Hallam • Haskell Harris • Robert Heuer • Myra Hines • Jeremy Holden • Jill Hudson-Neal • Dana Hughens • Bob Humphreys • Jessica Hundhausen • Donna Jenigan • Barbara Karth • Ani Kasten • David Keeps • Gayle King • Lisa Knapp • Lisa Kravet • Katherine Lagomarsino • Michael Lassell • Phyllis Lichtenstein • Luis Lobo • Roman Luba • Jack Lynch • Ann Maine • Mitra Mamdouhi • Mary Ann Mancini • Errick McAdams & Camsie Matis • Joe McCarthy • Sherry Moeller • Sungho Moon • Dee Mulligan • Dan Mulvena • Robin and Lorraine Murray • Lisa Newsom • Bill and Erin Nieder • Linda O'Keeffe • Maggie O'Neill • Candace Ord Manroe • Mitchell Owens • Jackie Patt • Katie Peters • Jimmy Rabette • Red Dirt Studio • Nedra Rhone • John Richardson • Jane Roberts • Patsy Rogers • Krissa Rossbund • Sabine Rothman • Michael Rufino • Robert Rufino • Karen Russell • Margaret Russell • Blaire Rzempoluch • Susanna Salk • Barbara Sallick • Peter Sallick • Rosa Sanjines • Eugenia Santiesteban • Anita Sarsidi • Suzy Slesin • Mark Smiley • Square Form Design • Michael Steinberg • Ed Teplitz • Jacqueline Terrebonne • Ryan Tessau • Meg Touborg • Newell Turner • Simon Upton • The Urban Electric Company • Richard Uza • Vilnis Vitols • William Waldron • Jordan Ware • Donna Warner • Nancy Webster • Lori Anderson Wier • Lenore Winters • Madame You

ACKNOWLEDGMENTS

To my clients and the countless people who have supported me over the course of my career, I truly thank you. To those I will inevitably forget, forgive me in advance if I have failed to acknowledge you. The second this manuscript goes to print, I will recall you and worry endlessly that I have alienated you.

Thank you, Trish Donnally, and your wonderfully supportive family, Robert and Danielle. Trish, your ever-watchful eye and constant care in helping my voice and thought process come through has so enhanced the articulation of my vision through this book.

Thank you, Gordon Beall, for your appreciation and understanding of the work. You have captured it brilliantly.

Special thanks to my comrades at Darryl Carter, for your constant attention to myriad details and for making things run with such precision. And ever more thanks to all of your partners, who I am SURE stopped you from quitting more than once.

Thank you, dear friends and counselors: Mary and Robert Haft (the embodiment of courage), and Penine Hart (you are your mother's stead; I have learned so much from you).

Thanks to all of you at Clarkson Potter for so much collective belief and support once again: Aliza Fogelson, Doris Cooper, Lauren Shakely, Pam Krauss, Marysarah Quinn, Jane Treuhaft, Rae Ann Spitzenberger, Tricia Wygal, Ashley Phillips, Kim Tyner, Kate Tyler, Kim Small, and Carly Gorga.

Thank you, Bob Barnett, Deneen Howell, and Alan Siegel (both as lawyer and therapist) for your wise counsel. And thank you to all of my friends at The Urban Electric Company . . . my friends at Benjamin Moore . . .

My thanks to all those mentioned in Appendix B, and to so many others, too numerous to name, but you know who you are.

And thank you to my supports: AA, GS / AB / AF, BG / AG / AH / AJH / AM / AMT / AOM / AS / AS, PD, R / ASU / ATF / BC / BCB / BF / BH / BQC / BR / BS / CB / CC / CEJ / CM, EM / EBS / DB / DC / DD / DF / DG / DH / DM, EM / DM / DS / DW / EA / EM / ET / GE / GG / GK / HH / IZ / JA / JAF / JB / JC / JG / JJA / JK / JM / JN, SM / JP / JR / JSD / KC / KC, GW / KD / KDP / KJR / KN / LD / LDF / LDR / LK / LMI / LN / LO / LR / MA / MAP / MAT / MB / MD / ME / MF / MH / MKL / ML / MM / MMG / MO / MP / MR / MRH / MS / MT / MVM / NB / NH / NL, JS / NS / NT / NW / PF / PH / PR / RM / RR / SC / SD / SDL / SF / SGM / SM / SQ, TB / SR / ST / SU / SV / SY, BG / TRL / TW / VM, SL.

And, of course, to Otis and Lucy, my ever-forgiving animals.

INDEX

Page numbers in *italics* refer to illustrations.